המדריך לטהרת המשפחה

The Concise Guide to
Jewish Family Laws

המדריך לטהרת המשפחה
The Concise Guide to Jewish Family Laws

A Guide
to the understanding
and observance
of the
JEWISH FAMILY LAWS

RABBI ZEV SCHOSTAK

First published 1971 Second edition, 1974
Third edition (revised and reset), 1983
Fourth edition (revised), 1993
Fifth edition (revised and reset), 2005
ISBN 1-931681-45-7

Published by
VTE
69-19 171st Street
Fresh Meadows, NY 11365
(718) 969-4828
Distributed by:
Israel Book Shop
501 Prospect Street
Lakewood, NJ 08701
Tel: (732) 901-3009 • Fax: (732) 901-4012
Email: isrbkshp@aol.com

Printed in the United States of America

משה פיינשטיין
ר"מ תפארת ירושלים
בנוא יארק

RABBI MOSES FEINSTEIN
455 F. D. R. DRIVE
NEW YORK, N. Y. 10002
OREGON 7-1222

בע"ה

הנה הרה"ג מהר"ר זאב מיימון שוסטאק שליט"א אשר אני מכירו לת"ח גדול ויורה לעומקה של הלכה והוא בקי
בהלכות נדה וחיבר גם ספר בלשון אנגלית כדי שידעו בנות ישראל שבמדינתנו היטב הדינים שצריכות לידע אך אי
אפשר היה לפני לעיין בספרו מפאת הלשון שאיני מכיר והעיקר מחמת שאי אפשר לעיין בכל דין ודין מצד קוצר
הפנאי ולכן לא אוכל להעיד על הספר אלא על המחבר שהוא בקי בהלכותיהן והוא חיבר הספר רק לשם שמים לזכות
את הרבים ויתברך הרב המחבר להתגדל בתורה ובכל המקצועות כברכת הבא על החתום בכ' טבת תש"ל בנוא יארק
נאום משה פיינשטיין

הנה הרה"ג מהר"ר זאב מיימון שוסטאק שליט"א אשר אני מכירו לת"ח גדול ויורה לעומקה של הלכה והוא בקי בהלכות נדה וחיבר גם ספר בלשון אנגלית כדי שידעו בנות ישראל שבמדינתנו היטב הדינים שצריכות לידע אך אי אפשר היה לפני לעיין בספרו מפאת הלשון שאיני מכיר והעיקר מחמת שאי אפשר לעיין בכל דין ודין מצד קוצר הפנאי ולכן לא אוכל להעיד על הספר אלא על המחבר שהוא בקי בהלכותיהן והוא חיבר הספר רק לשם שמים לזכות את הרבים ויתברך הרב המחבר להתגדל בתורה ובכל המקצועות כברכת הבא על החתום בכ' טבת תש"ל בנוא יארק

נאום משה פיינשטיין

ספר זה מוקדש
לזכר נשמות הורי

אבי מורי
אלקנה בן הרב זאב אריה ע"ה

אמי מורתי
חנה פרומעט בת רב אלימלך ע"ה

תהיינה נשמותיהם צרורות בצרור החיים

. . . .

A Special Tribute
to
my dear cousin
JEROME SCHOSTAK
for his wise counsel, personal interest in the
publication of my writings, and generous assistance.

May the Almighty bestow upon him and
his wonderful family His blessings for good health,
happiness, and continued success
in all their endeavors.

contents

. . . .

PART TWO: CONCEPTS

Preface

. . . .

Many misconceptions of the true meaning of the Jewish family laws have arisen nowadays. Due to our society's emphasis on the psychological motivation of our everyday conduct, many in our ranks tend to be highly self-conscious regarding laws which so directly affect their most intimate relationship. In an age when it has become fashionable to criticize almost everything, religious postulates are first in the line of fire.

It is for these reasons that the author felt the need to include a rationale of the Jewish family laws in this guide. It is of utmost importance that an authoritative guide on Jewish family laws also present the profound insights of our Torah into the reasons for our observance of these laws.

Of particular interest to both the general reader and the scholar are the annotations and footnotes found throughout the text. The source of each law in *Yoreh Deah* and later authorities is noted on each page of the text. Detailed explanations and source material of interest to the general reader are written in English, whereas references to responsa literature and original comments on the laws are recorded in Hebrew.

This guide is not intended to replace a class conducted in these laws, nor competent personal instruction in this subject. It is intended only as an up-to-date source book of the Jewish family laws and, as such, it should be reviewed occasionally so that all the laws will remain vivid in the reader's memory.

It should also be mentioned at the outset that the author has in no way attempted nor intended to make any legal decisions about the laws contained in this guide. Rather, he has endeavored to record, as accurately as possible, the generally accepted decisions of HaRav HaGaon, Rav Moshe Feinstein, with whom the author consulted frequently and at length concerning the numerous and varied aspects of these laws.

The author is also greatly indebted to the many competent rabbis and scholars whose comments and criticisms were invaluable in the preparation of this text. The author particularly wishes to express his gratitude to Mrs. Clara Glasser, Mrs. Hadassah Prero, Dr. Richard E. Broth and Dr. Harvey Lozman for their technical assistance in this project.

Note to the fifth edition
. . . .

I am much indebted to Rabbi David Cohen and Rabbi Shimon Eider, outstanding halachic scholars, whom I consulted frequently and at length in connection with this work. Their wide-ranging erudition, practical comments, warm friendship and patience, were a source of encouragement to me.

In addition, I am most grateful to Shlomo Nussbaum for his devoted efforts in totally reformatting this new edition and in enhancing its aesthetics. I am particularly indebted to Moshe Kaufman of Israel Book Shop, distributor of this Guide, for his invaluable suggestions and ongoing support.

Finally, my thanks to the many rabbis and educators who have recommended this Guide as a standard authoritative work on the Jewish family laws in the English language.

May the Almighty bestow His blessings on these wonderful people, and may they be numbered among those whose meritorious efforts for others bring merit on themselves:

מגלגלין זכות על ידי זכאי

Adar, 5765 (2005)   *Zev Schostak*

I

. . . .

טהרת המשפחה
הלכתה

*The Jewish Family Laws
in Practice*

. . . .

AUTHOR'S NOTE

In the following chapters, the reader is often advised to consult with a halachic authority. The need for a cordial, ongoing relationship between the layman and the expert who rules on halachah is of utmost importance. In fact, this unique relationship should be established and maintained for several reasons. First of all, halachah governs every sphere of Jewish life and an authority is often consulted in such diversified areas as *kashruth,* mourning and the family laws. Secondly, the pertinent problems involving application of Jewish law in our complex, technological society require the halachic expertise and practical knowledge of one who is frequently engaged to rule on these problems. Also, since quite frequently personal factors are considered in a halachic problem, the authority should be familiar with the one who poses the question. Finally, the intimate nature of the family laws can be more readily broached to an authority with whom one has already established a rapport.

One should always feel free to consult with an authority about even the most intimate problem — as each case will be treated objectively and in strictest confidence, in accordance with the highest standard of halachic ethics. Particularly, because an authority's religious scruples and piety are beyond question, any question may be posed without hesitation.

A Brief Summary of the Family Purity Laws

When a woman menstruates she is rendered a *niddah* (נדה). From the commencement of menstruation until after the woman immerses herself, at least twelve days later, she is considered to be a *niddah*. During this time, sexual relations are forbidden as are intimacies inciting to such relations. The prohibitions restricting intimacies during the *niddah* period are referred to as safeguards (דיני הרחקה).

The minimal twelve-day period is divided into several stages. The first stage of the actual flow comprises a set minimum of five days, even if the flow or staining has ceased before this time. However, if the flow or staining exceeds the five-day minimum, this stage is extended accordingly. On the afternoon after the termination of the flow (i.e. not before the afternoon of the fifth day), the *niddah* makes a thorough internal examination to ascertain that the flow has stopped. This examination is referred to as the interim of purity examination (בדיקת הפסק טהרה). If this examination is satisfactory, the final stage of the seven clean days (נקיים שבעה) begins. For seven consecutive days, the *niddah* must be clean of any blood or stain which can be attributed to menstruation. On the evening after the seventh clean day (i.e. not before the evening after the twelfth day), the *niddah* immerses herself in a special bath. This bath is referred to as a *mikvah* (מקוה) or ritualarium. Once a successful immersion is completed, the *niddah* period is concluded and sexual relations may be resumed.

CHAPTER ONE

When Does a Woman Become a Niddah?

$\cdot \cdot \cdot \cdot \cdot \cdot \cdot \cdot \cdot \cdot \cdot \cdot \cdot \cdot \cdot \cdot \cdot \cdot \cdot \cdot \cdot$

1. The Torah (Leviticus 18:19) prohibits sexual relations with a woman during her *niddah* (menstrual) period. When she discovers a red or black colored menstrual stain on her body or clothing, she is considered to be a *niddah*.[1] However, if she feels as if her period has begun, and upon checking immediately afterwards, finds nothing but a white discharge, she does not become a *niddah*.[2]

    She is also a *niddah* if she finds even a minute spot of blood on her examination cloth (see Glossary) or, under certain conditions, if she discovers a menstrual stain on her white clothing or sheets (קפג א, קצא).

2. The *niddah* period is not less than twelve days altogether. It comprises a set minimum of five days before the interim of purity examination[3] (even if the flow or staining has ceased before this time) and seven clean days after this examination. Of course, if the flow or staining exceeds the five-day minimum, the period is extended accordingly. The

period ends with a proper immersion in a *mikvah* and until the immersion is completed she is still considered to be a *niddah*.

(רמ"א קצו סוף הל' יא, קצז הל' א)

3. Even a minute spot found on an examination cloth[4] renders one a *niddah*. However, stains found on white undergarments or linen render one a *niddah* only when they cover at least an area the size of a penny[5] (קצ הל' ה לג).

4. The halachic definition of blood includes discharges, stains and spots of all shades of red or black.[6] White fluids or discharges are not included. However, yellow or brown shades require consultation with a halachic authority (קפח הל' א).

5. Even the aforementioned red or black stains *do not* render a woman a *niddah* if she finds them on colored clothing or sheets.[7] Thus, she is advised to wear colored undergarments and place colored sheets on her bed at all times (except on the seven clean days).

6. If one discovers blood in her urine or attributes her flow to an injury, sore, or operation, a halachic authority should be consulted.

7. At times, a doctor's internal examination may render one a *niddah* (see Chapter Ten).

1. ע' בש"ע קצ הל' א'.

2. פתחי תשובה שם, ס"ק ה, ו.

3. See p. 37-38.

4. Even in cases where the stain appears to be of an obviously menstrual nature, a halachic authority should still be consulted as it may be possible to attribute these stains to other factors.

5. מפי הגר"מ פיינשטיין זצ"ל.

6. See note 4.

7. והטעם כיון דדיני כתמים מדרבנן, לא גזרו על בגדי צבעונים. Pastel colored sheets are not included in this category (מפי הגר"מ פיינשטיין זצ"ל).

CHAPTER TWO

Laws Concerning the Bride Before the Wedding

· · · · · · · · · · · · · · · · ·

1. In order to prevent the wedding date from coinciding with the *niddah* period, the wedding date should be set in consultation with a halachic authority.

2. Every bride is considered to be a *niddah*. Thus, every bride is required to purify herself before the wedding. This purification consists of an interim of purity examination, seven clean days and an immersion. (see Chapter Five concerning details of these laws) (קצב הל' א, וש"ך ס"ק א).

3. The bride should begin the interim of purity examination early enough to allow the immersion concluding the seven clean days to occur no later than the night before the wedding. For example, if the wedding is scheduled for Wednesday night, the interim examination should be made at least eight days earlier — on Tuesday afternoon. Thus, seven clean days will elapse before the immersion occurs on the Tuesday night before the wedding.

Many rabbis recommend that the interim of purity examination be made still earlier (e.g. on the ninth or tenth day before the wedding) to allow leeway in case complications arise. Naturally, in this case, the seven clean days and the immersion are advanced accordingly. However, the immersion should not precede the wedding by more than four days[1] (קצב הל' ב).

4. The immersion should take place at night.[2] However, if the wedding occurs on the evening following the seventh clean day, the bride may immerse herself during the day, providing the ceremony will take place when it is definitely nighttime (קצז הל' ג' רמ"א שם, סד"ט, ודגו"מ, ופמ"א).

5. If the wedding occurs during the period when the bride is considered a *niddah*, the bride and groom must sleep in separate rooms[3] with chaperones. The bride should be chaperoned by a female and the groom by a male (a halachic authority should be consulted as to the ages of the chaperones). During the daytime, they should also be chaperoned by someone when alone.
(רמ"א קצב הל' ד, ח"א, וחזון איש, יו"ד סי' צ"א).

6. If the wedding has been postponed, even if the bride has counted seven clean days, a halachic authority should be consulted (קצב הל' ג, וש"ך שם).

---

1. If the immersion unavoidably occurs more than four days before the wedding, the bride should check for clean days from the immersion until the first relations (רמ"א קצב הל' ד).

2. Night is established by the appearance of three medium-sized stars. The immersion should take place at least 30 minutes after sunset (מפי הגר"מ פיינשטיין זצ"ל).

3. באמת דין דבשני חדרים אינם צריכים שימור, המובא ברמ"א בשם הרשב"א צ"ע. ע' בלשונו של הרשב"א בב"י סוף סימן קצב דמתיר רק בשני בתים. ולפי"ז בשני חדרים בבית אחד אסורים להתיחד. ושמעתי מפי הגר"מ פיינשטיין זצ"ל דבשני חדרים בבית מלון אסורים להתיחד בלי שומרים.

CHAPTER THREE

Laws Concerning the First Relations
· · · · · · · · · · · · · · · · ·

1. Consummated relations[1] with a virgin[2] render her a *niddah*. Once the marriage has been consummated, the bride must count a total of eleven days. In this case, the seven clean days begin on the fifth day after the marriage has been consummated[3] (קצג הל' א).

2. Immediately after the marriage has been consummated, the bride and groom may sleep together in the same room, but in separate beds. All other safeguards of the period apply (see Chapter Four) from this time until the immersion on the evening of the eleventh (קצג הל' א).

---

1. Full penetration in coitus, even though blood cannot be found, renders the bride a *niddah*. Partial penetration may also render the bride a *niddah*.

2. Virgins are strongly advised against using tampons, internal protection, or from making vaginal examinations before the wedding other than those prescribed, as this often destroys the hymen (מפי הגר"מ פיינשטיין זצ"ל).

3. Compare with the clean-day period in other cases (see p. 19) which begins no earlier than the sixth day after the flow.

CHAPTER FOUR

Safeguards of the Niddah Period
· · · · · · · · · · · · · · · · ·

1. Human sexual nature may be easily aroused and stimulated in the intimacy of the marital relationship. Hence, the Rabbis were empowered by the Torah[1] to institute safeguards to prevent intimacy during the *niddah* period when relations are forbidden[2] (רא"ש סוף נדה בקיצור הלכות נדה, מובא בעה"ש ס' קצה).

2. One should not touch his wife during the *niddah* period.[3] In order to prevent touching, the couple should not hand or throw[4] articles to each other. Thus, any article they wish to transfer must first be placed on a surface by one mate and then picked up by the other (קצה הל' ב).

3. A husband should not *drink* from his wife's leftovers, unless someone else partakes of her leftovers beforehand, or the leftovers are removed to a different cup. He should not *eat* from his wife's leftovers even if they are removed to a different plate.[5] A wife may eat or drink of her husband's leftovers (קצה הל' ד).

    The couple should not eat directly from the same plate. Rather, portions should be served from the main platter to the individual settings (ט"ז קצה ס"ק ב).

Specific applications of these two above laws are:

(a)   Meat should first be divided into portions on the serving platter, and then served to the individual table settings.

(b)   A large loaf of bread may be sliced and distributed to the family. However, small bread rolls should not be shared by the couple since they are baked for the consumption of one person and will result in the husband's eating of his wife's leftovers (which is forbidden).

Similarly, beverages may be shared by the couple only when served from large containers. Beverages served from small containers (e.g. small soda bottles normally consumed by one person) should not be shared by the couple.[6]

(c)   Butter may be taken from the same dish by both husband and wife.[7]

(d)   If there were different types of food on the *niddah*'s plate and she ate only of one type, the other types are not considered her leftovers and the husband may partake of them.[8]

4. A *niddah* should not pour beverages or serve food to her husband in the normal manner. Rather, she should serve in a different manner than usual (e.g. by serving with her left hand or by placing the food farther from her husband than usual) (קצה הל׳ י).

5. The couple should not sit down to eat by themselves without placing an article on the table between them that is not used during the meal. For example, they may place a vase or napkin holder that is normally kept elsewhere on the table. Alternately, they may use different placemats, different tablecloths, or one may eat at the bare table while the other uses a tablecloth. In lieu of these alternatives, they may eat together at the same table if another person sits with them (קצה הל׳ ג).

6. A husband should not sit on or sleep in his wife's bed, even if she isn't present.[9]

7. The couple may not sit down together on any seat or surface where the weight of one may affect the other, such as a bed or a couch with only one cushion. Accordingly, they may sit on a couch with two cushions (רמ״א קצה הל׳ ה).

8. They may travel together in a motor vehicle because

the vibrations of the seat result from the movement of the vehicle and not from the weight of the passengers. However, they should sit apart from each other, and it is advisable that they place a purse or package between them to serve as a buffer.[10]

9. Since during the *niddah* period the couple is not allowed to sleep in one bed, when buying furniture or renting a furnished apartment, they should secure separate beds. During the *niddah* period, the beds should not touch each other (קצה הל' ו).

10. It is preferable that a *niddah* not sing in the presence of her husband.[11]

11. It is suggested that the *niddah* wear a different type of apparel (e.g. an apron) as a reminder of this period (קצה הל' ח).

12. A *niddah* should not prepare the sheets and pillowcases of her husband's bed for sleeping, in his presence. However, she may make the bed in his presence as the bed is made as part of the housekeeping routine[12] (קצה הל' יא).

13. A *niddah* should not prepare her husband's bath, or pour water directly on his hands[13]

(קצה הל' יב, וש"ך ס"ק טז).

14. When a woman is a *niddah*, her husband may not gaze upon the parts of her body which are normally not revealed (קצה הל' ז).

15. The couple should refrain from discussing sexual topics during this period (קצה הל' א, וש"ך שם ס"ק ב).

16. When the husband is sick and there is no one to take care of him, the *niddah* is permitted to attend to his needs, providing she does not wash his face or body and does not prepare his bed in his presence. However, when she is ill, a halachic authority should be consulted on the question of who may care for her[14] (קצה הל' טו, טז).

---

1. Tractate Yebamoth, 21 a, based on Leviticus 18:30.

2. Leviticus 18:19.

3. It is also advisable that one refrain from touching the clothing that his wife is wearing (ע' פ"ת, קצה, ס"ק ג).

4. ע' פ"ת קצה ס"ק ד, דיש להתיר אם יזרוק דבר למעלה ולא לנוכח אשתו והיא פושטת ידה ומקבלתו. וע' מה שהביא שם בשם הס"ט להחמיר.

5. שמעתי מפי הגר"מ פיינשטיין זצ"ל דאין לבעל לאכול משיורי מאכלה
של אשתו גם אם יניח אותם על קערה אחרת. וכן מובא באגרות משה
י"ד ס' צ"א, דליכא תקנה בכה"ג. ונכון לציין כאן דהאיסור לאכול
דוקא משיוריה הוא שיודע שהם שיוריה. ואם אינו יודע שהם שיורה
ורוצה לאכלם אינה מחוייבת להגיד לו (ע' בעה"ש קצה ס"ק יא).

6. אגרות משה י"ד, ס' צב.

7. Ibid.

8. אגרות משה, י"ד, ס' צא.

9. ערוך השלחן ס' יח. וע' בח"א, קטז, ס' ה, דמיקל דוקא בישיבה.

10. אגרות משה, י"ד, ס' צא.

11. ע' פ"ת קצה, ס"ק י. אמנם שמעתי מפי הגר"מ פיינשטיין זצ"ל
דאם כי מוטב שלא תשיר, אין לאסור.

12. וכן שמעתי מפי הגר"מ פיינשטיין זצ"ל. והרבה טועים בזה וסוברים
שלא תסדר מטתו בפני כלל. והנכון דדוקא הצעת המטה, דהיינו פריסת
סדינים והמכסה, היא שנאסרה, דהוי דרך חיבה, ולא סידור המטה,
דהוי בכלל עבודת הבית.

13. ע' בעה"ש קצה ס"ס י"ד, דמתיר לה להביא או לשפוך מים אל
הכלי. אולם בש"ד ס"ק טז וח"א אוסרים.

14. ע' פ"ת קצה ס"ק טו. ולענין אם הולכת נדה לבית הקברות ע' פ"ת
ס"ק יט.

CHAPTER FIVE

Laws Concerning the Niddah Period
· · · · · · · · · · · · · · · · ·

The total *niddah* period, beginning with the flow and culminating with the seventh clean day, must be at least twelve days in duration. This period is divided into three stages: (I) the days of the flow or staining; (II) the interim of purity examination; (III) the seven clean days.

I. THE DAYS OF THE FLOW OR STAINING

The days of the flow (ימי הראייה) comprise the first stage of the *niddah* period. When a woman senses the passage of a liquid from her womb, as she does when she normally menstruates, or she discovers a stain (see Chapter One for details of these laws), her *niddah* period has begun. The first stage of this period, the days of the flow, is not less than five days altogether (even if the menstruation or staining has ceased before this time). However, if she menstruates for more than the five days, this stage is extended accordingly (רמ"א קצו הל' יא).

The *niddah* should mark the days of her flow on her personal Hebrew calendar. In addition, she should note whether the beginning of the flow occurred during the daytime or during the night. (See Chapter Seven for details of how future periods are calculated). Then she counts four additional days after the first day of the flow. Thus, if one becomes a *niddah* on a Saturday night[1] or on a Sunday afternoon, she may first make the interim of purity examination Thursday afternoon.

II. INTERIM OF PURITY EXAMINATION

On the afternoon of the fifth day *well before sunset* the *niddah* is required to inspect herself thoroughly for any trace of blood. This examination is referred to as the interim of purity examination (הפסק טהרה) because it marks the interim between the flow and the seven clean days. After the examination is satisfactorily completed the seven clean days begin (שבעה נקיים).

There are several important laws related to this examination:

(a)   It is of utmost importance that the examination and its preparations begin well before sunset. If, however, for some unavoidable reason, she examined herself a few minutes after sunset, a halachic authority should be consulted.[2]

(b)   If the examination occurs on a Friday afternoon,
      it should preferably be made before the Shabbos
      candles are kindled (i.e., 18 minutes before sun-
      set). In the summer, where some congregations
      recite the *maariv* (evening) service much before
      sunset, one may be advised to make the exami-
      nation once before the *maariv* service and again
      before sunset (ע' בח"א, קיז ה).

(c)   The purpose of the examination is to determine
      that the flow has definitely stopped and thus it
      is usually made in the following manner:

> Stained underpants should be removed.
> The vaginal area is then thoroughly
> washed.[3] A very soft and pliable white
> cloth is wrapped around the index finger
> and inserted deep into the vaginal tract.
> Then the cloth[4] is moved around in all the
> internal folds and crevices and removed.
> If a stain is found, this procedure may be
> repeated with a clean cloth if there is still
> time before sunset. Consequently,
> sufficient time should be allotted before
> sunset for this contingency. Once the cloth
> has been checked under daylight before

sunset and no stain has been found, the
examination is satisfactory.

It is strongly recommended that the cloth be rein-
serted tightly into place and then left there, preferably
for about forty minutes after sunset, but at least for thir-
teen and a half minutes after sunset.[5] Since the cloth
penetrates as deeply as possible for this time, many
women lie down while the cloth remains inserted to
prevent any discomfort. Once the cloth is checked the
next morning and not even a minute stain is found, the
examination has been proven satisfactory.

If this examination proves unsatisfactory, it is
repeated in the afternoon. This examination may be
repeated on successive afternoons until the results are
proven satisfactory.

III. THE SEVEN CLEAN DAYS

The completion of a satisfactory examination signifies
the beginning of the seven clean days (שבעה נקיים).
For seven consecutive days, one must be clean of any
blood or stain which can be attributed to menstruation.

There are several important laws pertaining to these
days:

(a) Throughout the seven clean days a woman should wear clean, close-fitting,[6] white[7]undergarments and have a clean, white sheet on her bed because menstrual stains found at this time could invalidate her count. If she is traveling or is in a situation where she cannot wash herself or her garment, or does not have a change of clothes, she should inspect her garment for stains (רמ"א קצו הל' ג).

(b) A woman should examine herself twice daily by daylight during the seven clean days.[8] If, for some reason, she was unable to examine herself each day, then she *must* examine herself on both the first and seventh days during the daytime (קצו הל' ד).

(c) The examinations for the seven clean days are generally made while one is standing, one foot raised on a chair to facilitate the insertions. A clean, white, pliable cloth is wrapped around the index finger and inserted deep into the vaginal tract. Then it is rotated in all the internal folds and crevices and removed (קצו הל' ו). Great care should be taken to see that the cloth is soft and pliable (e.g., a piece of white cotton or linen that has been washed at least once in the laundry) and that the examination is made very gently and carefully to prevent causing internal bleeding. After the cloth is checked by daylight and found to be clean of any stain, the examination is satisfactorily completed.

(d) If a woman has a flow or sees a stain[9] during the seven clean days, she must repeat the interim of purity examination and count the seven clean days anew, but need not repeat the five days (קצו הל' י).

(e) If a woman errs by counting less than five days of the flow or less than the seven clean days, and consequently immerses herself earlier than the prescribed time, a halachic authority should be consulted (ועי' בעה"ש קצו סי' מא).

---

1. It should be noted that in Jewish Law night is considered part of the following day. Hence, even if one becomes a *niddah* on Saturday night, the five-day period begins on Sunday and the examination cannot be made before Thursday afternoon.

2. שמעתי מפי הגר"מ פיינשטיין זצ"ל, כי בשעת הדחק יש להקל אם

בדקה בתוך שמונה דקות (מינוטין) לאחר שקיעה.

3. Those women who douche for internal cleaning should wait about ten minutes after the douche is completed until they begin the interim of purity examination (מפי הגר"מ פיינשטיין זצ"ל).

4. Cotton balls are not recommended because they tear or shred easily in the process.

5. השיעורים שמעתי מפי הגר"מ פיינשטיין זצ"ל. Two minutes should be added to these times if they are based on sunset found in most newspapers. Thus, the cloth should be left in place for at least 15½ minutes but preferably for 42 minutes after sunset.

6. Close-fitting undergarments are very important
(מפי הגר"מ זצ"ל פיינשטיין).

7. If the *niddah* forgot to change from her colored undergarments and found a stain, a halachic authority should be consulted.

8. Women who are newly married and experience pain when making the examinations during the clean days should consult a halachic authority.

9. See pp. 21-22 concerning the stains that render one a *niddah*. If any stain is found, a halachic authority should be consulted.

CHAPTER SIX

Laws Concerning Immersion

I. THE TIME FOR IMMERSION

After the seven clean days are concluded, the next step is immersion. The immersion should take place immediately after the seventh clean day. Until the immersion is completed properly, one is still considered to be a *niddah*. One should be most careful that the immersion take place at night, at least 30 minutes after sunset[1], in a reliable *mikvah* (ritualarium)[2] (קצז הל' א).

1. If a woman's husband is in the city, she should not delay going to the *mikvah* at the prescribed time. If for some reason she wishes to postpone the immersion or schedule an immersion for the eighth day during the daytime, a halachic authority must be consulted (קצז הל' ד).

2. If the time for immersion occurs on a Friday night, one may go to the *mikvah*. Even if the immersion was to occur on Thursday night and for some unavoidable reason, it did not take place, one may

immerse herself on Friday night. Similarly, if the immersion on Thursday night was found to be invalid, one may immerse herself on Friday night (רמ"א קצז הל' ב).

3. If the immersion occurs Friday night, preparations[4] for immersion must be made before Shabbos.[5] If Thursday and Friday are holidays and the immersion is scheduled for Friday night,[6] preparations for the immersion must be made on Wednesday afternoon (קצט הל' ה, ו).

4. When the immersion will occur on a Saturday night, or after the conclusion of a holiday, one is forbidden to make these preparations in the afternoon preceding the immersion. Thus, one should wash herself and comb her hair thoroughly before the Shabbos or holiday and once again before the immersion. In this case, one should also avoid touching sticky foods when preparing the festive meals. Thus, it is suggested that one wash her hands after the preparation of these meals (קצט הל' ד, ו).

5. One should postpone the immersion if it will occur on Yom Kippur, Tisha B'Av or during the seven days of mourning. However, preparations for the

seven clean days or the immersion (e.g., washing the lower extremities slightly with her hands, wearing clean clothing, etc.) may be made even during these days.[7]

II. ADVANCE PREPARATIONS BEFORE IMMERSION

The principle of immersion is that the whole body should be immersed in the water at one time, and that every part of the body should be in direct contact with the water. Hence, any separation (חציצה) between the skin and the water renders the immersion invalid. Consequently, any dirt, cosmetics, food or paint stains, threads and pins in the hair, jewelry, etc., must be removed before immersion. Details of these laws will be treated in this section (קצח הל' א).

1. Among the articles that are separations: hair bands and hairpins, rings, earrings and bracelets (קצח הל' ב). Bracelets, necklaces, rings and earrings are only separations when they are so tight that water cannot enter between them and the skin. If one forgot to remove such jewelry and immersed herself, another immersion is required. However, loosely fitting jewelry which permits contact between the skin and water is not considered a

separation. Consequently, if one forgot to remove such jewelry and immersed herself, another immersion is not required (קצח הל' כג).

2. Hair[8] should be combed thoroughly and all braids and knots should be loosened and untied. If any knots are found tied in the hair after the immersion was completed, a halachic authority should be consulted (קצח הל' ה).

3. Underarm and pubic hair should be cleansed thoroughly and separated (קצח הל' ו).

4. The glutinous substance usually found in the corner of the eye should be removed. However, if one forgot to remove it and is unable to repeat the immersion, the immersion is valid (קצח הל' ז, ש"ך, י"ג).

5. Contact lenses should be removed before the immersion. However, if one forgot to remove them, and immersed herself, the immersion is valid and a second immersion is not necessary.[9]

6. Bandages, band-aids or casts[10] on a wound are considered separations (קצח הל' י).

7. Wounds, cuts or scratches, where a scab has developed, or which are more than three days old and

the pus has dried, should be soaked in water until they become soft (קצח הל' ט).

8. A sliver or thorn which penetrates into the skin is a separation if it protrudes above the outer layer of skin or is level with the skin. However, if it penetrates below skin level, even though it is still visible, it is not a separation (קצח הל' י"א).

9. Blush or other facial cosmetics, where the cosmetic substance has been entirely removed and only the cosmetic's coloring remains, is not a separation. Similarly, inks, dyes, or paints where the substance has been removed and only the color has penetrated into the skin pigment (and cannot be removed with soap and water) are not separations.[11] In all cases the skin should be scrubbed thoroughly with soap and water, and nail polish should be completely removed.

10. Women should carefully clean and trim their nails before immersion (קצח הל' י"ח). If one forgot to trim a nail and immersed herself, she must immerse herself again. However, if after returning home and engaging in relations, she discovered that a nail was not trimmed before immersion, a halachic

authority should be consulted[12]
(רמ"א קצח הל' כ, ט"ז וש"ך שם).

11. Toenails should also be cleaned and cut. However,
if one forgot to trim them and immersed herself,
another immersion is not necessary if the woman
in question doesn't object to their not being
trimmed[13] (פ"ת קצח ס' י).

12. If the immersion occurs on a Friday night and one
forgets to trim her nails Friday afternoon, she may
ask a gentile woman to trim them. On the intermediate days of a holiday (חול המועד) one may trim
her nails herself (עה"ש קצח ס' מט).

13. All split or hanging nails and all cuticles should be
trimmed. Hanging cuticles or nails which are only
minutely split are not considered separations
(ח"א קיט, טז).

14. If a finger is so swollen that the nail cannot be
trimmed or manicured and the dirt beneath the nail
cannot be seen due to the swelling, there is no separation (קצח הל' יט).

15. One should brush her teeth and clean between
them with a toothpick or dental floss before

immersion to remove any food particles that may have lodged there. In order to prevent meat particles from lodging between the teeth, women customarily abstain from eating meat within the day prior to the immersion. However, if the day prior to the immersion is Shabbos or a holiday, they may eat meat[14] (קצח הל' כד וט"ז).

16. If the immersion occurs on Friday night, and one forgets to clean her teeth Friday afternoon, she may clean her teeth with dental floss and with a tooth-brush without toothpaste.[15]

17. A permanent dental filling or a temporary filling, which is properly made, is not a separation. However, a loosely-fitting temporary filling may be a separation and a halachic authority should be consulted.[16]

18. Braces which grip the teeth tightly are not a separation if their function is to prevent the teeth from falling out. However, if their function is to beautify (i.e. to straighten) the teeth, they must be loosened or removed before immersion.[17]

19. Partial plates and full dentures should be removed

for immersion.[18] A partial bridge that cannot be removed is not a separation (ח"א קיט, יח).

20. Although the Torah requires that the water of the *mikvah* contact only the external parts of the body, the water should be able to enter the internal areas as well. For this reason, one must cleanse her mouth, nostrils, ears, navel, anus and genitals as well as the skin folds of her body.
(קצט הל' א וחכמת אדם קכא ס' א)

21. If one did not cleanse her internal areas and finds a separation in any of these areas after immersing herself, another immersion is required (קצח הל' כה).

22. One should be careful not to knead dough, touch wax, or come in contact with any adhesive substance on the day before the immersion (רמ"א קצח הל' כד).

23. If one is weak and needs support to immerse herself, her friends or a woman who supervises the *mikvah* may dip their hands in the water and, without removing their hands from the water,[19] gently hold her. However, they should not grip her tightly. They should also let go of her for a second when she is immersed, if she is able to stand up without assistance (קצח הל' כח).

III. FINAL PREPARATIONS BEFORE IMMERSION

1. Before immersing, the woman should wash every area of her body from head to toe with soap and warm water. She should comb her hair thoroughly, removing all knots and braids. Then she should make a final check to see that there are no separations on her body. The woman supervising the *mikvah* may aid her in checking for separations that are not visible to her (e.g., on her back). In case the woman makes the cleansing preparations in her home, she should keep her body meticulously clean until immersion (קצט הל׳ א, ב).

2. If she did not comb her hair and check her body for a separation, even though she finds no separation after immersion, she must make these preparations and immerse herself again. However, if she forgot to check the internal areas of her body and did not find a separation after the immersion, she does not have to immerse herself again[20] (קצט הל׳ ח, ט).

3. She should not eat between the washing preparation and the immersion (רמ״א קצח הל׳ כד).

4. If she forgot to check for food particles between her teeth and immersed herself and afterwards

discovered a particle there, another immersion is necessary (ש"ך קצח ס"ק לג).

5. She should check for any dirt on her feet, particularly at the bottom of her feet
(קצח הל' מה, וח"א קכא ס' א).

6. The aforementioned preparations should take place late in the afternoon while it is still day and continue until the nighttime when the woman may immerse herself. If it is difficult to make the preparations during the day, or the immersion occurs immediately after Shabbos or a holiday,[21] the preparations should be made carefully and without haste in the evening (קצט הל' ג, ד).

7. If she must attend the lavatory, she should do so before immersion (רמ"א קצח הל' מג).

IV. THE PROCEDURE OF IMMERSION

1. After all the preparations are completed, the woman should descend into the *mikvah* to the level where the water is at least a foot above her navel.[22] Then she should bend forward until her head and hair are beneath the water. She should hold her arms

and feet slightly away from her body, as in walking. She should not press her lips or eyelids together tightly, nor clench her fists. However, she may close them naturally (i.e. without pressure), if she wishes. She should not crouch too much or stand erect in the *mikvah* when she is in position for immersion (קצח הל׳ לה, לו, לח, לט).

If the water is not high enough for her to immerse while standing (i.e., if the water will not cover her whole body), she should lie flat on her back or stomach (or lie on her side) beneath the water (ס׳ פה קצח הל׳ לז, עה״ש קצח).

2. If she held her lips together too tightly during the immersion, another immersion is required because the water could not come in contact with her whole lip or mouth. However, if she forgot and closed her eyelids too tightly, a halachic authority must be consulted[23] (קצח הל׳ לח, לט).

3. It is the responsibility of the woman supervising the *mikvah* to see that all of the woman's hair and body is beneath the water during the immersion (קצח הל׳ מ).

4. If the *niddah* is in doubt whether her hair was

beneath the water, the immersion is not acceptable
(ח"א, קכא, ס' ד).

5.   After immersing once in the water, a woman
should stand erectly, eyes upward, arms folded beneath the heart, and recite this blessing:

בָּרוּךְ אַתָּה ה' אֱלֹקֵינוּ מֶלֶךְ הָעוֹלָם, אֲשֶׁר קִדְּשָׁנוּ
בְּמִצְוֹתָיו וְצִוָּנוּ עַל הַטְּבִילָה.

She should then immerse herself again in the water (סימן ר, וע' בבאר היטב שם בשם השל"ה).

6.   After the immersion is completed,[24] a woman's first
contact should be with another woman. As a matter
of modesty, a woman who has attended the *mikvah*
should be discreet and not disclose her visit to anyone but her husband.

---

1. שיעור זה שמעתי מפי הגר"מ פיינשטיין זצ"ל.

2. Immersion is valid only in a ritual bath containing 40 *se'ah* of
undrawn water. Thus, only a properly constructed *mikvah* is valid
for immersion and not a bathtub or swimming pool. One must consult a halachic authority if she wishes to immerse herself in a lake or
stream, because some of them are man-made. She should always
ascertain the reliability of a *mikvah* in a place which is not familiar.

3. ע' בעה"ש, קצז, ס' ח, דמתיר טבילה בליל שבת בכל ענין.

4. See pp. 37-40 for details of these preparations.

5. One who immerses herself on Shabbos should not wring out her hair or towel after drying herself.

6. In all cases where the immersion will occur on a Friday night, the wife may light the candles and recite a blessing over them well in advance of sunset. However, she should make a condition that she will not accept the Shabbos or holiday until after she has finished preparing herself for the immersion (ע' במ"ב ס' רס"ג ס"ק י"א, כ"א).

7. ע' משנה ברורה, תקנא, ס"ג, לענין כיבוס בגדים ולבישת לבנים מר"ח אב עד תשעה באב. ולענין רחיצה ולבישת לבנים באבילות וט"ב ע' בשער הציון שם, ס"ק ל"ה. ולענין רחיצה ולבישת לבנים ביום כיפור' ע' במ"ב תרי"ג ס"ק ל"א.

8. Dandruff is not a separation.

9. אגרות משה, י"ד, ס' ק"ד.

10. מפי הגר"מ פיינשטיין זצ"ל.

11. ע' בעה"ש, קצח, ס' מג: כל דיו דאין בו ממש הוי כצבע שהנשים צובעות על פניהם ולא הוי חציצה.

12. ע' שם דנחלקו הט"ז וש"ך אם שכחה ליטול ציפורן ולנה עם בעלה אם צריכה טבילה אחרת לדעת הט"ז אינה צריכה טבילה אחרת שלא להוציא לעז על הטבילה. והש"ך חולק. וע' בעה"ש קצח ס' מח ובח"א קיט ס' יד.

13. ע' פ"ת שם. אולם בעה"ש קצח ס' מח כתב ומ"מ צ"ע למעשה. ושאלתי את פי הגר"מ פיינשטיין זצ"ל, והורה דאם אינה מקפדת יש להקל.

14. Similarly, if one attends a wedding or Purim *seudah* prior to the immersion, one may eat meat at the wedding meal or Purim *seudah*, providing that her teeth are cleaned well before the immersion

(מפי הגר"מ פיינשטיין זצ"ל). Women also abstain from eating chicken within the day prior to the immersion (חיים' קצח ס' כד) (מקור).

15. אגרות משה, א"ח, ס' קיב. One should be careful not to wet the toothbrush.

16. אגרות משה, י"ד, ס' צז.

17. אגרות משה, י"ד, ס' צו.

18. If one forgot to take out removable false teeth before the immersion, another immersion is required (מפי הגר"מ פיינשטיין זצ"ל).

19. ע' בעה"ש, קצח, ס' סא.

20. However if she forgot to check and then after the immersion finds a separation in an internal area, she should immerse herself again (ש"ך קצט ס"ק יט).

21. Some of the preparations (e.g. washing and combing) are made before and after the Shabbos or holiday, see p. 54.

22. This distance is calculated from the measurement of a זרת (the span between the little finger and the thumb of a spread hand). This measurement is also equivalent to 3 טפחים (fist-breadths), which are 9 inches, according to some authorities; 12 inches according to others (פ"ת קצח, ס"ק כא).

23. ע' בש"ך שם, ס"ק נא, שאינו חושש לטבילה בדיעבד אם עצמה עיניה ביותר. וע' עוד בח"א, קכא, ס' יא ובעה"ש קצח, ס' פו.

24. שמעתי מפי הגר"מ פיינשטיין זצ"ל, דמותרת להתרחץ תיכף אחר טבילתה, ואינה צריכה להמתין עד שתבא לביתה.

CHAPTER SEVEN

Laws Concerning the Expected Menses
· · · · · · · · · · · · · · · · · ·

In order to calculate future menses (וסתות) one should note on her Hebrew calendar whether her flow[1] began during the day[2] or night and on which dates[3] her flow occurred.

The couple must abstain from sexual relations[4] during the day or night when the menstrual flow is expected. For example, if one's last flow began during the afternoon, the couple must abstain from relations during the day of the expected menses. They should also abstain from relations the day or night before the expected flow.[5] For example, if the flow is expected during the day, the couple should also abstain from relations the night before (קפד הל' ב).

A woman should also examine herself during the time of the expected flow.[6] This examination is the same as the one made during the seven clean days (see p. 41).

The date or dates when the future periods may occur are calculated according to a woman's menstrual cycle. There are two types of cycles: irregular and regular.

I. IRREGULAR CYCLES

Most women do not have a set day each month when their menstrual flow invariably begins. For example, a woman may begin to menstruate on the 28th, 29th, and 31st day of three consecutive months. In most cases, where the period is irregular and a set cycle[7] has not been established, one must assume that her period may begin at *all* of these following times:

1. Thirty days from the beginning of the last period. For example, if the first day of the period is on Wednesday, the period may be expected on Thursday of the fifth week hence[8] (קפט הל' א).

2. The date on the Hebrew calendar that the last period began.[9] For example, if the period began on the third day of Elul, the next period may be expected on the third day of Tishre (קפט הל' ב).

3. The interval between menses. For example, if the interval between the first day of her last period and the first day of her present period is 29 days, her next period may be expected 29 days hence (קפט הל' ב).

In addition to the three aforementioned methods for calculating future periods, there is another method for predicting the onset of a period. If one invariably experiences headaches, cramps, yawning, or various pains prior to menstruation, these symptoms indicate the commencement of a new period and a halachic authority should be consulted for direction (קפט הל' יט).

Taking the three aforementioned calculations into consideration, a sample irregular cycle is:

I.   If one's first recorded menses occurred on the 19th of Nisan, she may expect her menses on:

1. the 18th of Iyar, which is 30 days after the 19th of Nisan (the 19th of Nisan is counted as the first of the 30 days).

2. the 19th of Iyar corresponding to the date of the month when the last cycle began.

II. If the woman in question, in fact, menstruates on the 19th of Iyar as anticipated, she may expect her next flow at the following times:

1. the 19th of Sivan which is 30 days after the 19th of Iyar (the 19th of Iyar is counted as the first of the 30 days).

2. the 19th of Sivan which also corresponds to the date of the month when the last cycle began.

3. the 20th of Sivan which is 31 days after the last period (counting the 19th of Iyar as the first of 31 days) and equivalent to the interval of 31 days between the first flow on the 19th of Nisan and the second on the 19th of Iyar.

III. If this woman, in fact, menstruates on the 10th of Sivan, next month's menses should be anticipated at the following times:

1. the 9th of Tamuz, which is 30 days after the 10th of Sivan.

2. the 10th of Tamuz corresponding to the date of the month when the last cycle began.

3. the 30th of Sivan which is 21 days after the last period occurred (counting the 10th of Sivan as the first of the 21 days) and equivalent to the interval of 21 days which elapsed between the 19th of Iyar and the 10th of Sivan.

II. REGULAR CYCLES

There are numerous ways of establishing a regular cycle, all of them based on the principle that a menstrual flow must recur three times in a specified pattern. This pattern may consist of regular intervals of the same number of days between four periods (e.g., 3 equal intervals of thirty days between the first day of four periods) or recurrence of the first day of the flow on the same date of three consecutive months (e.g., the eighth day of Tishre, Heshvan and Kislev). Due to the fact that there are a number of patterns besides the aforementioned, many of which are very intricate, a halachic authority should be consulted in establishing a regular cycle and for details about observance of that cycle.[10]

---

1. Menstrual staining found on clothing and/or linens (and not on a pre-checked examination cloth) is not considered acceptable criteria for establishing any cycle and one need not expect future periods to begin on the same date that one stained in the past (קצ' הל' נד).

2. Day begins at sunrise and ends at sunset. Night begins at sunset and ends at sunrise. באמת יש להחמיר שיום מקרי מעמוד השחר
וע' בעה"ש קפד ס' כז.

3. Even though expected menses are generally calculated from the first day of the flow, some authorities and various customs establish a regular cycle based on other days of the flow. Thus, all the days of the flow should be noted on the calendar.

4. המחמיר בשער קריבות, כגון חיבוק ונישוק, תע"ב. אולם, לדינא מותר
ש"ך, קפד ס"ק ו.

5. יש לחוש לחומרת הא"ז לפרוש מאשתו גם בעונה הקודמת לוסת ש"ך, קפד, ס"ק ז.

6. ע' קפד הל' ט, וע' בח"ד ס"ק כב דמבואר שם דבדיקת הוסת היינו בדיקת חורין וסדקים, כגון בדיקת ז' נקיים. ולמנין הבדיקות מצריך מרן הגר"מ פיינשטיין זצ"ל, שתים.

7. Examples of set cycles are the recurrence of the first day of the menses on the same date of three consecutive months (e.g., the eighth of Tishre, Heshvan, and Kislev) or three consecutive intervals of the same number of days between four periods (e.g., three intervals of thirty days between the first day of four periods).

8. Some authorities are of the opinion that 31 days is the correct calculation. Thus, if the period begins on Wednesday, the period may be expected on Friday of the fifth week.

9. All dates are calculated according to the Hebrew (lunar) calendar. Some months are full months, comprising 30 days; other months comprise 29 days. The months comprising 30 days are: Tishre, Shevat, the first month of Adar in a leap year, Nisan, Sivan, and Av. The months always comprising 29 days: Tevet, the month of Adar in a regular year and the second month of Adar in a leap year, Iyar, Tammuz and Elul. The months Heshvan and Kislev sometimes number 29 days and sometimes number 30 days.

10. For a helpful *halachic* website to calculate expected menses, go to www.torahsoftware.org, and download Vestos.

CHAPTER EIGHT

Laws Concerning Pregnancy and Childbirth

· · · · · · · · · · · · · · · · ·

1. One who has ended the third month of her pregnancy does not have to anticipate her period until after childbirth.[1] If one does see blood after the third month, the laws of an irregular cycle[2] apply and a regular cycle cannot be established. During the first three months of pregnancy, all the laws of irregular and regular cycles still apply (קפט הל' לג, לד).

2. A woman who gives birth or miscarries, whether to a live or stillborn child or an embryo, becomes a *niddah* with the onset of labor.[3] If the child is a boy, one may make the interim of purity examination as soon as it is feasible,[4] count seven clean days, and then immerse herself. However, if one gives birth to a girl or miscarries a girl, she must count fourteen days, making the interim of purity examination on the seventh day. Hence, the last seven days of the fourteen days would be counted as the seven clean days and one may immerse herself at their conclusion (קצד הל' א).

3.   If a woman miscarries after 40 days of the pregnancy
     and the sex of the child is undetermined, one must
     count fourteen days as in the case of giving birth to
     a girl (קצד הל' ב, ג וש"ך ס"ק ג). (If she miscarries
     before 40 days, she is, of course, rendered a *niddah*.)

4.   If a child is delivered through a caesarian section
     and no blood is emitted from the vagina, the mother
     of this child does not become a *niddah* and does not
     have to count any days or immerse herself[5]
     (קצד הל' יד).

5.   If twins are delivered, particularly if one is a boy
     and the other is a girl, the order and times of birth
     should be noted and a halachic authority should
     be consulted for direction
     (קצד הל' יג, ועה"ש קצד ס' מט, נה).

6.   After the childbirth,[6] the mother's regular cycle is
     re-established on the same date it was established
     before pregnancy. However, if she had an irregular
     period before the pregnancy, the dates calculated
     from that cycle are no longer valid
     (קפט הל' לד, ופ"ת קפט ס"ק לב).

7.   When a woman reaches menopause, a halachic
     authority should be consulted for direction
     (קפט הל' כח, כט).

1. Hence, after the third month, a couple need not abstain from sexual relations on dates established before the pregnancy, because the flow has ceased.

2. One authority maintains that the 30-day period (see p. 60) does not apply here; others state that it does apply. A halachic authority should be consulted for direction.

הס"ט מובא בפ"ת, קפ ט ס"ק לא, כתב שאינה צריכה לחוש לעונה בינונית. אולם, החוות דעת ושו"ת חסד לאברהם חוששין לעונה בינונית.

3. In the case of false labor, if the pains have ceased and no blood is emitted from the vagina, one does not become a *niddah*

(ע' פ"ת קצד ס"ק ח, ועה"ש, קצד ס' נג).

4. Usually women stain for several weeks after childbirth.

5. If a boy is born of a caesarian section he may not be circumcised on Shabbos and he is exempt from redemption of the firstborn

(יו"ד, רסו ס"ק י, ש"ה ס"ק כד).

6. Following childbirth, a nursing woman can establish a regular cycle.   שמעתי מפי הגר"מ פיינשטיין זצ"ל, שמינקת קובעת וסת.

CHAPTER NINE

Laws Concerning Contraception
· · · · · · · · · · · · · · · · ·

The first commandment in the Torah is the propagation of mankind: "Be fruitful and multiply." The significance of this commandment is not measured only by its being the first of the 613 commandments. It takes precedence over many other commandments because of its ultimate importance.[1] It is the only commandment in the Torah where both man and his Creator participate. The Talmud states, "There are three partners in the creation of man — man, woman and the Holy One, Blessed be He."

Since this commandment is vital, it should not be thwarted or postponed for the purpose of convenience, financial or otherwise. Only in cases where one's health and well-being were adversely affected did the Talmud permit contraception.[2] Even in these cases, one should consult with a halachic authority as to the method of contraception.[3]

The use of any contraceptive measure should not be decided by a husband and wife on their own. They must *always* consult with a halachic authority who will determine if their individual case merits the use of contraceptive measures. Among the factors an authority will consider in the evaluation of each case are:

a. The couple should have complied with the commandment to "be fruitful and multiply."

    In order to fulfill the minimum requirement of this commandment, they should be parents of both a boy and a girl.[4]

b. The method of contraception is a major factor. There are several well known contraceptive measures:

    I.   Surgery. Operations made for the purpose of sterilization (i.e. vasectomies in the male and tubal ligations or hysterectomies in the female) are generally forbidden, except in rare situations.[5]

    II. Intrauterine contraceptive devices, medical authorities believe, speed up propulsion of the egg in the tube, preventing fertilization; or if fertilization takes place, make conditions unfavorable for implantation. Condoms placed on the male organ and diaphragms used with spermatocidal jellies raise major questions in halachah about wasted semen.

These forms of contraception are generally forbidden and a halachic authority must be consulted.[6]

III. Rhythm system. This method, based on the fact that conception does not usually occur after 48 hours from ovulation have passed, proposes that sexual relations do not take place within the 48 hours after ovulation. Aside from the well-known ineffectiveness of this system (due very often to the problems of calculating the date of ovulation and the discipline involved in abstinence from sexual relations before[7] and after ovulation), it is not uncommon that the preferred period for sexual relations coincides with the *niddah* period. This system is devoid of the problems of the aforementioned methods of contraception. However, as in instances where the use of the other contraceptive measures is contemplated, a halachic authority should be consulted.[8]

IV. Contraceptive pills (estrogen/progesterone) and transdermal patches present at least two major problems in halachah. Research reveals that a small number of women on the pill discovered increased staining between periods that they never experienced before taking the pill. Naturally, this staining can cause additional *niddah* periods[9] (see p. 42). Moreover, according to F.D.A. studies, there is some risk to the health of certain women who take the pill. Since the Torah admonishes one to protect his health, contraceptive pills present difficulty in this regard too. Depo provera injections and micronor pills, which are progesterone-based, present issues of break-through bleeding. Again, the husband and wife must be cautioned to consult a halachic authority when considering use of any contraceptive.

c. The physical and psychological conditions of the woman in question[10] or her future offspring,[11] is also of major importance in determining whether a contraceptive measure is to be used.

---

1. For example, a Torah scroll may only be sold to enable one to learn Torah or to marry, Megillah 27a.

2. Yebamoth 12b, Ketuboth 39a.

3. במקום סכנה התירו האחרונים שתכניס טבעת עמוק בתוך רחמה בכדי שלא תתעבר. וע' יותר בענין זה בספר חזון איש, אה"ע, הל' אישות, אחיעזר, ס' לז, שו"ת חלק א, ס' כג, וחלק ג, ס' כד, אגרות משה, אה"ע, ס' סג, סד.

4. אה"ע א, הל' א, ה, וע' שם הל' ח, שיש בזה גם חיוב דרבנן.

5. See Tractate Shabbos 110b.
וע' באגרות משה, אה"ע, ס' יג, סו, בדיני סירוס באשה.

6. וע' בשו"ת אחיעזר, חלק ג, ס' כד, ואגרות משה, אה"ע, ס' סג.

7. Since the sperm may be viable for up to 72 hours, even relations occurring a day or so before ovulation can fertilize the egg, which is viable up to 48 hours after ovulation.

8. ע' באגרות משה, אה"ע, ס' קכב, ריש ס' קכב, אם מותר לדלג הימים שיכולה להתעבר ולבעול בימים שאינה יכולה להתעבר לפי דעת הרופאים.

9. ע' באגרות משה, אה"ע, חלק ב, ס' יז, דמבואר שם מה צריכה האשה לעשות בכדי לברר שהיא מאלו הנשים שאינן רואות דם מזה.

10. ע' באגרות משה, אה"ע, ס' סה, לענין אשה שנשתטית אחר הלידה והרופאים אסרו לה להתעבר, ושם ס' סז, ברוצה לישא אשה שהיא חולה שאסורה לה להתעבר.

11. ע' באגרות משה, אה"ע, ס' סב, בענין נתינת מוך וסם לח לאשה קודם תשמיש מצד מחלה שנולדים ילדים חולים.

CHAPTER TEN

Laws Concerning Visits to a Doctor
· · · · · · · · · · · · · · · · ·

1. One who visits a gynecologist or obstetrician who
    makes an internal examination of the vaginal tract
    with his fingers need not suspect that the womb was
    touched in the examination and that it consequently
    discharged any blood.[1] However, if the doctor in-
    serted an instrument into the vaginal tract, he
    should be asked about the width of the instrument
    and the depth of insertion and these facts should
    be presented to a halachic authority.[2]

2. If a doctor inserts an instrument into the vaginal
    tract, but claims that it did not touch or enter the
    womb, the woman does not become a *niddah.*[3]

3. If a doctor performs a dilation and curettage of the
    uterus (D and C), one becomes a *niddah.* However,
    if he takes a Pap smear, a halachic authority should
    be consulted.

4. In order to avoid the aforementioned problems that
    might result from an internal examination,
    cleaning, or test, one should confine her visits to

the gynecologist or obstetrician to the days of her
flow, if possible.

5. If a couple has not had children after many years
    of marriage and the doctors suggest that by
    advancing the date of the immersion[4] a day or two,
    conception will be more likely, or if they advise
    tests of the sperm,[5] or artificial insemination,
    stringent prohibitions are involved and only
    halachic experts should be consulted.

---

1. An established principle in the Talmud is that it is impossible
for the womb to open without discharging blood. However, in this
case, since one's fingers do not reach the womb, we do not suspect
that the womb opened. שו"ת מהרש"ם, ח' ב, ושו"ת ח"ס, ס' קעט.
ושמעתי מפי הגר"מ פיינשטיין זצ"ל, שאינה צריכה לבדוק את
עצמה לאחר בדיקת הרופא.

2. יש מחלוקת אחרונים בדין הנודע ביהודה. וע' בעה"ש, קפח, ס' נא,
פ"ת, קצד, ס"ק ד, ואגרות משה, י"ד, ס' פט.

3. ה"ה אם רופא זה אינו שומר מצות (מפי הגר"מ פיינשטיין זצ"ל).

4. ע' בשו"ת דובב מישרים, ס' ח, וע' באגרות משה, י"ד, ס' צג, באיסור
שהצריכו ז' נקיים במקום פו"ר.

5. וע' בשו"ת אחיעזר חלק ג, ס' כד, ובאגרות משה, אה"ע, ס' ע, וח"ב, ס' ט"ז.

טהרת המשפחה
השקפתה

Concepts of
the Jewish Family Laws
· · · · · · · · · · · · · · · · ·

CHAPTER ELEVEN

Insights into the Torah's Views on Love
· · · · · · · · · · · · · · · ·

Today's society paints a picture of love which is incongruous with the Torah's concept of love. The media convey the view that youth "falls in love" before marriage, implying that this attraction is based more on chance than on choice. In this storybook-type romance, the young woman and man are somehow mutually attracted, and because this mystic attraction, or love, magically hides any faults that either one may possess, they cannot help but live happily ever after. As this attraction is primarily physical, the physical proximity of the partners is the chief catalyst in the development of their relationship. This chance attraction is the love that is preconditional to marriage.

The Torah portrays love in a different light. Love evolves more from choice than chance. The Torah, as we shall see, defines love as a rational process, elevating physical love above the mundane sexual drive to one of the supreme forms of human expression. It is constantly growing, developing after marriage even more than before marriage. This is because genuine love is essentially based on rational recognition and appreciation of another being's nature, and this comprehension of another's nature is possible only in the framework of a marriage. Ultimately, since the Torah emphasizes the rational nature of love over the physical, the constant physical proximity of the two lovers is not necessary to sustain and stimulate the relationship.

LOVE = KNOWLEDGE – THE EQUATION OF MARITAL BLISS

Throughout the Torah, we find a relationship between love and knowledge. Rationality, as we have seen, is not only exercised in seeking love when *choosing* a mate; rather in the Torah, we find that it is synonymous with love.

In the Book of Genesis (18:19), the Creator accords Abraham recognition for his unquestioning loyalty by stating: *"For I know him, that he will command his household after him, and they shall keep the way of the Lord."* Rashi comments on this verse that the words "For I know him" are an expression of affection. He cites various examples of the Hebrew word דעת (knowledge), all of which denote affection. Rashi thus concludes that the words meaning love and knowledge are related because "one who loves another brings him close and knows and recognizes him."

Later, in Genesis (24:67), the Torah relates that Isaac's love for Rebekah developed only after their marriage. "And Isaac brought her into the tent of Sarah his mother, and took Rebekah and she became his wife, and he loved her, and Isaac was comforted after his mother's death." In this verse, the Torah clearly delineates the sequence of events. First Rebekah became his wife and then he loved her and was comforted. The Ramban (Nachmanides) observes the sequence of this verse and comments:

> Onkelos explains the verse in this manner: "Isaac brought her to the tent and behold she was Sarah, his mother. Isaac's love is mentioned here for because of her (Rebekah's) righteous abilities he loved her and was consoled."

In other words, only after Isaac married Rebekah did he recognize her righteousness and many other good qualities. Only after Isaac *knew* of these qualities did he love her. Only because he knew her did he realize that she embodied the values of his mother and he was comforted after his mother's death.

Another analogy of love through recognition and

knowledge is man's love for his Creator. The Rambam (Maimonides) writes of this love:

> What is the path that leads to man's love and reverence for the Creator? When man contemplates His wondrous and manifold deeds and creations and sees in them His immeasurable and infinite wisdom, man immediately loves, praises, glorifies and greatly desires to know Him.
>
> *(Mishneh Torah. Hilchoth Yesodey HaTorah 2:2)*

Not only does knowledge inspire love but, in essence, knowledge is love. Thus, we find that the Torah employs the term "Adam knew Eve, his wife" (Genesis 4:1) in reference to their sexual relationship. Knowledge is synonymous with love.

In the final analysis, since genuine love is rational in essence, it will be as meaningful and enduring as knowledge itself. However, sensual love, by virtue of its physical nature, can only be transient and temporal. The Mishnah expresses this thought:

> All love dependent on sensual attraction will pass away as soon as the sensual attraction disappears;

but if it is not dependent on sensual attraction, it will never pass away.

(Mishnah Avoth 5:19)

LOVE—A LIVING CONCEPT

As we have seen, the Torah equates sexual love with knowledge, ". . . and Adam knew Eve, his wife." In marriage, this love through knowledge is a profound form of human expression. This knowledge is not only knowing the other's personality, but also, is the ability to exercise self-control. Since man can rationally control his sexual drives, his love is meaningful; but his love is even more meaningful because he has the ability to abstain from expressing it. An animal cannot abstain from reproduction. It is bound by its instinctual drives. But man, by virtue of his will and intelligence, can control his sexual drives. Since man may refrain from sex, when he does express love, it is an autonomous act, rather than a mere instinctual response. In short, in man's right to refuse, he has been granted a right to choose.

The Jewish family laws are living expressions of this concept of love. During the period of separation, a couple voluntarily abstains from sex, but this does not in any way diminish their love. On the contrary, when they choose to express love, it is filled with mutual respect. During this period of separation each mate learns to respect the sexual rights of the other. At this time, abstinence is a must, necessitating control over one's drives. At this time, as always, the other's feelings must be respected. The period of separation also teaches the couple that sex cannot be denied without reason. It is not a toy to be denied as a threat or punishment, nor should it be given as a reward. Only because the Torah makes abstinence imperative during the *niddah* period must a normally healthy couple practice such an extended period of abstinence.

Perhaps, more than ever before, the couple will realize at the conclusion of the *niddah* period that the conditions of sexual practice mentioned in the Torah have one common purpose—the development of mutual respect for another's sexual rights. This purpose is apparent in many laws of the Torah. For example, if relations were allowed during the menstrual period, the sexual rights of the woman would be violated. It is a well-know fact that many women are physically weaker during their period and some experience menstrual cramps or depression. Relations under these conditions could be a threat to the physical and psychological well-being of the woman.

There are other instances where the Torah protects a woman's sexual rights. For example, the Torah forbids a husband to have relations with his wife when there is a substantial suspicion that she has committed adultery. Similarly, the Talmud advises a husband to abstain from sexual relations when he is seriously considering divorce. In both of these cases, the husband probably detests his wife and would be "using" her only for his own sexual gratification. Since the mutual respect underlying the sexual relationship does not exist in these cases, abstinence is the prudent course.

It has often been asked: Don't the frustrations of not being able to touch during the *niddah* period impair a couple's love? The answer: In the mature, rational relationship that is love, physical proximity is not the only factor. A couple's ideals, beliefs, and goals are much more important factors in their love. By observing the Jewish family laws, a couple proclaims their belief in the Torah and learns that there is more to marriage than sexual intimacy. Their beliefs and goals transcend any momentary pleasure they may derive by violating these laws. In complying with their common beliefs and goals, they will find that they have inner reserves of self-control. Even newlyweds who may find it difficult to practice abstinence will find that they have great willpower and self-restraint. As time passes, they will have as little desire to violate the safeguards of the *niddah* period as they do to smoke a cigarette on Shabbos. Young couples who are self-conscious about their observance of the *niddah* safeguards, especially in the presence of others, will find that this self-consciousness will also fade away. As time passes, they will realize that others are not staring at them, prying to discover if they observe the *niddah* laws. Other people are not really that concerned. Thus, a couple's observance of the *niddah* safeguards will blend naturally into their daily routine.

Another question that is often asked is: How can a husband and wife express love during the *niddah* period when they cannot touch? The answer: They will discover new ways to convey their love. A wistful glance, a reflective thought, or a favor to ease the other's everyday tasks, are also tender expressions of love. They will learn that silence and self-restraint are often more eloquent than kisses and caresses. They may even develop new interests and hobbies that they can share with each other during the *niddah* period. The rational expressions of love will outlast the physical aspects and truly deepen their love and commitment to each other and their beliefs. Above all, they will recognize that their love is as enduring now as it was before, even though it has found new modes of expression.

CHAPTER TWELVE

Concepts of Defilement and Purity

When a *woman* has her menstrual period, she is considered to be impure until she immerses herself in the *mikvah* (ritualarium). Upon immersing herself, she returns to her original state of purity. During the time of her impurity, however, sexual relations are forbidden—as are intimacies inciting to such relations. Since impurity is the source of sexual prohibitions, some women have developed negative feelings about this concept. They consider this period as taboo! Under this taboo, they must voluntarily turn off their sexual feelings and impose excessive self-control—all because of natural physiological processes over which they have no control. Subconsciously, these women may feel rejected because they are "impure," and they feel denigrated.

In reality this approach is actually based on misconceptions about the essence of defilement and purity. Defilement and purity are totally spiritual concepts, and cannot be equated with innate "evil" versus "good," or rejection as opposed to acceptance. If one were to review all the instances of defilement mentioned in the Torah (i.e. contact with the deceased;

creeping insects; seminal emissions; menstruation, etc.) he would find that they all have one thing in common — all involve an involuntary act over which one has little or no control. Rabbi Samson Raphael Hirsch, the renowned German thinker and leader, makes a most enlightening observation about this phenomenon. Hirsch says that the highest state to which man can aspire is a rational one in which he can exercise voluntary control over his being and environment. Since defilement results from involuntary acts or uncontrollable physical processes, it can only be understood as Divine limitation on man's autonomous self-dominion.

In light of this revealing and inspiring new insight, it is obvious that defilement is not a taboo or an inherently negative concept. Rather, it is a reminder of our own physical limitations and the possibility of attaining an ideal state of rationality and self-determination.

Another *raison d'être* of these laws delves into the symbolism of defilement and purity. The defilements mentioned in the Torah relate, in some way to death. For example, a priest may not enter the room of a corpse and then serve in the Temple. In other words, contact with the deceased prohibits him from performing the life-sustaining function of atonement. A leper is also considered to be defiled. His plight evolves from the death of certain skin tissue on his body. Similarly, seminal emissions or menstruation involves a loss of "life" — the wasted seed of a potential human being. Thus, the Torah in its profound reverence for life, requires water—the source of life—to overcome defilement, the symbol of death. Only natural water, as symbolized in the waters of the *mikvah,* can offset the forces of death and bring about a state of purity synonymous with life!

In this context, we again see that defilement is not a mystic taboo. Rather, it alludes to death in its broadest sense.

According to all views of defilement, it is clear that we are dealing with spiritual concepts, unrelated to physical uncleanliness or psychological rejection. Purification in a *mikvah* does not guarantee that a woman will become meticulously clean or more attractive to her husband. As Maimonides writes: "Defilement is not dirt or filth which can be removed by water but is, rather, a Divinely-ordained law. . ." (*Mishneh Torah, Mikvaoth* 11:12). Purity (טהרה) and impurity (טומאה) are but spiritual concepts and, thus, it is only fitting that they be understood

to connote *spiritual* purity and *spiritual* impurity.

CHAPTER THIRTEEN

Medical and Psychological Benefits of the Family Purity Laws

CANCER PREVENTATIVE

Many women are pleasantly surprised to find that observance of the family purity laws offers many positive side benefits. For example, medical studies at New York's Mount Sinai Hospital indicate that Jewish women who observe the family purity laws are much less subject to cancer of the uterus than is the rest of the population. The findings of many leading gynecological specialists also substantiate this conclusion. For this reason, many gynecologists and obstetricians feel that the Pap smear does not have to be administered to women who observe *niddah.*

HEALTH PROTECTION

It is also a well-known fact that many women are weaker during their monthly period and experience menstrual cramps and/or mild depression. Indeed, research studies of 40 million women suggest that about 90% experienced varied hormonal changes about the time of their period. During the separation of husband and wife for the duration of the *niddah* period, their sexual energies will be restored. Observance of the family purity laws allows a full recovery to a vigorous state of health.

SEXUAL RENEWAL

Many psychologists feel that there are certain times when a woman's sexual drive recurs more frequently than during other times. Certainly the *niddah* period, a time when many a woman's sexual desire is at low ebb, is an appropriate time for abstinence. Naturally, the conclusion of this period, which has been anticipated by both husband and wife, is an ideal time for resuming sexual relations.

The need for renewal of sexual desire is not limited to woman. In today's society, sex has become mundane. It has been degraded from a warm, human relationship to a mechanical act. Man has so taken for granted this act that he, too, needs something to renew his sexual desire. He must have a stimulant to restore the warm, personal and esteemed relationship that he once enjoyed. This stimulus is given to man through the observance of the Jewish family laws.

"Because a man may become overly familiar with his wife and thus repelled by her, the Torah said that she should be a *niddah* for seven clean days (after her flow) so that she will be as beloved (after her period) to her husband as on the day of her marriage" (Tractate *Niddah* 31b).

This statement attests to the fact that every husband and wife who practice the laws of family purity find constant sexual renewal throughout their marriage. Since they abstain each month from sexual relations, these relations, when permissible, will be more appreciated and enhanced. Their relationship will never be taken for granted. Their marriage will be a perpetual honeymoon — "a wife will be as beloved to her husband as on the day of the marriage."

THE ULTIMATE REASON FOR OBSERVANCE

Now that a rationale of these laws has been presented, one should always remember that the medical and psychological advantages of these laws are only side benefits. In the final analysis, we observe these laws because we fully accept the Torah's commandments, whether or not we fully comprehend the reasons for observance. As a matter of fact, since the Jewish family laws are based on the concepts of purity and defilement, we may never really fathom their meaning because these concepts were revealed on Mount Sinai as statutes (חקים). This means that, like the laws of *kashruth*, the Torah offers no reason for their observance. Yet, we commit ourselves to these laws as we do to laws which we do comprehend. We comply with the laws of *niddah* and *kashruth* just as we do not steal or kill. We do not violate a law just because we do not understand it. We realize that our comprehension, compared to Divine intelligence, is limited. We recognize that the Creator, in His infinite wisdom, saw fit to ordain these laws, and He knows why they are necessary and beneficial. Thus, we practice the family purity laws with full confidence in His judgment.

CHAPTER FOURTEEN

Chesed — the Key to Compatibility

The Hebrew word *chesed* (חסד) denotes hospitality or kindness, but actually connotes selfless devotion beyond that which is required by the Torah. Wherever we find *chesed* mentioned in the Torah, it implies much more than social etiquette. *Chesed* is not a mask worn merely as a social amenity. Rather, it is an integral part of one's personality. One who possesses this characteristic naturally thinks of others before himself. And it is this quality of *chesed*, selflessly caring for another human being, that is a key to compatibility in the marriage relationship.

The Torah relates that *chesed* filled Abraham's being and motivated his many acts of hospitality. Even when he was recuperating from his circumcision, he sat outside his tent in the scorching heat, looking for guests. Despite his discomfort, he ran to extend an invitation to the three strangers who passed by his tent. Without thought for his condition, he personally served a meal to these men and did not ask a servant to wait upon them. This incident reveals that Abraham was not hospitable to strangers because the Torah compelled him to be kind. The Torah, in fact, exempts an ill man from this *mitzvah*. Similarly, he was not hospitable merely because of social etiquette. He could have complied with social etiquette even if his servants had attended to the strangers. Yet, Abraham did more than he was required and personally waited upon his guests because hospitality was his nature. He so enjoyed serving his guests that he did not feel any discomfort from his operation. *Chesed* was an integral part of Abraham's nature, and he transmitted this trait to his descendants, the Jewish people.

When seeking a mate, the quality of *chesed* ranks among the most important considerations. Two people who genuinely care for each other above and beyond what is expected of them have a solid foundation for a good marriage. Thus, the Torah rates this quality as an essential prerequisite to marriage. When Eliezer, Abraham's loyal servant, searched for a mate for his master's son, he looked for one characteristic — *chesed*. With this quality, he undoubtedly felt, a girl would be most compatible with Abraham's family. In order to discover the girl who possessed this quality, Eliezer proposed a test. The girl who would not only offer him to drink, but would also attend to his camels would exemplify *chesed*. Rebekah, as it turned out, graciously served Eliezer *and* his camels. Social etiquette obliged Rebekah only to pour Eliezer a drink of water. But, her *chesed* compelled her to do more than what was expected — to attend to his camels as well. Thus, Eliezer knew that Rebekah was a worthy choice for Abraham's son.

Throughout our history, we find outstanding personalities who were models of *chesed.* One of these was Ruth, the devoted convert to Judaism. When young Ruth expressed her interest in marrying the elderly Boaz, he replied, "Blessed be thou. . . my daughter, for thou hast shown more kindness (חסדך) in the last instance than the first, by not going after the young men, whether they be poor or rich." The question has been raised — what kindness did Ruth display by marrying Boaz? After all, Boaz was one of the most highly respected men of the community and very wealthy. Ruth would really have been doing herself a favor by marrying a man of such repute and means. Yet, Boaz considered marriage to Ruth a special kindness on Ruth's part.

The answer is that marriage demands a measure of devotion, something that Ruth possessed in abundance. Marriage, by nature, requires that one's personal considerations often be put aside in favor of the ultimate benefit of the family unit. This quality of considering another before herself, Ruth had always amply displayed. For example, when Ruth and her mother-in-law, Naomi, had lost their husbands, Ruth refused to forsake Naomi as her sister-in-law, Orpah, had done. Ruth was so devoted to her mother-in-law, that she automatically put aside any possibility of remarriage. Yet, she remained steadfast in her devotion. In Ruth's conversion to Judaism she bravely chose to walk a rocky path, rejecting the security of her own people. Despite the loneliness and insecurity Ruth may have felt, she fully committed herself to the Torah. Again, we have an instance where Ruth's *chesed* precluded her own personal needs. Her selfless devotion to others, her total commitment to her deepest beliefs, are the main characteristics of *chesed*. Thus, Ruth's marriage to Boaz was really a kindness (*chesed*) and a favor to *him*.

This devotion to her beloved, which so typifies a young bride, is praised in the Prophets. The Creator compares the loyalty of the Jewish people during the exodus to that of a bride: "I remember the kindness (*chesed*) of your youth, the love of a young bride who followed after Me in the desert in an unsown land."

Did the Jewish people know how they were going to be housed and fed in the desert? Did a nation of over 600,000 people consider what they would eat in the barren desert that awaited them? Yet they trustingly followed their Master into the desert, like a bride who follows her husband, despite her fears of the unknown. In this way, the Jewish people exemplified the supreme value of *chesed*—sacrifice above self-concern.

A husband also expresses *chesed* in the marriage relationship. Before he marries, he has no one in particular towards whom he may direct his *chesed*. He has not found anyone with the sensitivity to appreciate his kindness. But, after he marries, this is changed. Now he has found the sensitive receiver for his love and affection. His wife and family become the focal point of his *chesed*. He lovingly provides his wife and family with their needs. He is the provider not only because he must do so by law. He is the provider because he wants to release his innate reserves of *chesed* towards those he loves the most. His inherent sense of devotion to his family impels him to take care of them. A husband's obligations to his family may be legal, but his commitments, filled with love and kindness, transcend these obligations.

Unfortunately, man today finds himself in a society which is the antithesis of *chesed*. He lives in a society of takers, not givers. The attitude of the average man is, "What's in it for me?" In this rat race, man quickly discovers the effects of this attitude. He finds himself in a highly self-centered contest where respect for human dignity and genuine concern for the welfare of others are old-fashioned values. Apathy is common, true empathy is rare, and self-sacrifice for others almost unknown. Of course, our social attitude leaves its mark on the average marriage relationship. Again and again young people ask, "What will I *gain* from the marriage?" Almost never does the conscience ponder, "What can I *give* to the marriage?"

This attitude, unfortunately, carries over in the sexual relationship. A man or a woman may be so obsessed with their own gratification, that the needs of the other partner are disregarded. Yet, the one who has been gratified feels he has done no wrong for he looks upon himself as the logical taker in the marriage. However, the Torah finds this partner morally guilty, for every Jew should be considerate of another's needs. Particularly in the sexual relationship, the Torah requires each husband to see to it that his wife is gratified. In this part of his life, too, the husband must be a giver.

In our era of indifference, we must learn to listen to others with compassion. In this age of apathy, we must learn to do for others with devotion. Now, more than ever, we must fan the flame of *chesed* that lies dormant in our hearts. We must take the key of kindness to unlock the door of marital bliss.

CHAPTER FIFTEEN

Man and Woman—
A Marriage of Heaven and Earth
· · · · · · · · · · · · · · · · ·

It truly staggers the imagination: Since the beginning of time, from all the trillions of mankind ever created, each of us is truly unique, unlike any other that has preceded us or that is living today. Our personal experiences, education, culture, innate character and personality traits are so distinctive that it is virtually impossible for others to be us, and act and react invariably as we would. Our uniqueness is, upon deeper reflection, the very reason for our existence. Had the Almighty wanted to merely populate the world with so many look-alike, act-alike humans, He would have created them as He did the animal kingdom: Multitudes of faceless clones, devoid of individuality. In a world of human clones, there would be no need for creative self-expression since there would be no self-identity. Fortunately, each of us was created as a one-of-a-kind personality, unique in the history of mankind, as an expression of our special role and mission in this world. "Just as their faces are different, so are their views," the Midrash

(*Tanchuma, Pinchos* 10) tells us. The fact that each of us is so special, that no one has ever been created like us, leads to another startling revelation: somehow the world would be incomplete, indeed, imperfect without our having been here. This may be why the Mishna concluded: "Every man must truly declare that this world was created for my sake!" (*Sanhedrin* 37a).

In the world of Jewish metaphysics, Kabbalah, this individuality of man is seen as a reflection of his spiritual core—his soul. This soul, *neshama, is* quite literally a breath *(nishima)* of the Divine Presence that has elevated man above the animal kingdom and plant life. In the epic of creation recorded in Genesis (1:20-31), only Adam was personally fashioned by God and received the Divine breath of life; all other animals were created according to their species, male and female, without any special distinction. Man, Adam, was originally created alone (Rashi 1:27) and appointed, as it were, the executor of God's new world. Man was created without a mate, just as God has no partner, to demonstrate that he was given total mastery over the physical universe, as God's proxy on earth (see Rashi 1:26: "If I do not create my counterpart [lit., one similar to me] in the lower worlds [i.e., the physical universe], then I will evoke jealousy among the creations"). At this point in creation, before Eve was formed, we pause to reflect about the true nature of man, for this was pristine man as he was meant to be. Man was originally a bisexual creature, possessing both male and female physical features and personality traits. Later, to counteract the impression that man without mate was akin to God, the Creator declared, "It is not good for man to be alone."[1] He then formed woman, not as a totally new creation, but rather by removing man's feminine features and personality traits from his being.[2]

We may conclude from this development that man in his pristine state was a God-like, self-contained creature, not requiring another being for self-perfection and perpetuation. Indeed, just as God, the quintessence of perfection, possesses both male and female traits, so did original man. Consequently, the ideal, or most natural state of affairs, is that of one being embodying both masculine and feminine qualities. In fact, Kabbalah projects images of God as manifestations of both these sexual roles. And this is as it should be, if we perceive Him/Her as the perfect, all-inclusive Creator who personifies all the diverse qualities of His/ Her creations — both male and female.

Man, as a self-contained, God-like proxy, was not meant to be.[3] Adam was divided into male and female counterparts like the rest of the animal kingdom, but with one crucial difference: His original, perfect state was that of a bisexual creature. This distinction suggests that man, in his relationship with woman, hopes to become one again with her and, in so doing, return to this ideal state. It also sheds new light on a passage in the Torah and a saying of the Rabbis. When God presents Eve to Adam immediately after she was created, Adam declares, "This time, bone of my bone, flesh of my flesh; this one shall be called woman for she was taken from man." Then the Torah, almost parenthetically, offers advice for all future generations: "Therefore, man should leave his father and mother and cleave to his wife and they shall become one flesh" (2:23-24). Rashi (ad loc.) notes that they become "one flesh" through the child born of their union. In light of our thesis, however, and in keeping with the flow of the text, we may understand this passage on a different level. After God removed Adam's feminine half to create Eve, Adam realized that he was no longer a complete, autonomous God-like being. Adam was crestfallen, for as the Rabbis put it, man is not whole without woman *(Yebamoth* 63a). Yet, when he bonds with her, they become, once again, one being — "one flesh and bone" — returning to the perfect condition of man — a Divine creature embodying both masculine and feminine qualities. Man now exults in joy that, in woman, he has discovered his true identity: at last, he has found his missing self. So the Torah urges every man who wishes to achieve self-actualization: "'cleave to [your] wife and become *one* flesh!" This also explains why, unlike animals, man is, natually monogamous.[4] Lower animals mate instinctively only to propagate their species. The males and females of each group have no fidelity to each other because they were originally formed as two separate creatures. Man, however, is faithful to his mate because man and woman were once one being. Now that they are rejoined in marriage, they become one again.

Actually, there is another dimension to the unique relationship of man and woman — the spiritual affinity of husband and wife. Man, as we have observed, has been endowed with a *neshama* — a breath of the Divine — imbuing him with a unique spiritual character and charging him with an exclusive mission in this world. Man is able to fulfill this mission only because he was blessed with two other exceptional gifts that distinguish him from other animals: man can *think* and *feel!* The well-known Aramaic translation of the Bible by Onkolos underscores man's greatness as an articulate being. On the verse "And man became a living creature," (Genesis 2:7), Onkolos renders: "And man had the power of speech." We recognize that man was not merely given the ability to communicate in modes similar to those which scientists have discovered among primitive life forms. Man was endowed with the entire cognitive domain — to imagine, reason, create, articulate, and express in art, music, speech and writing. He was also imbued, at creation, with the ability to feel, which is another uniquely human quality. While lower life forms have various innate or natural instincts, such as the maternal instinct of a mother to care for her babies, no other creature has the range or depth of emotions and feelings possessed by man. From the depths and despair of depression to the resplendent heights of joy and ecstasy, man experiences and expresses what no other being in this world can. Man thinks and feels. He dreams, envisions, explores,

designs, loves, laughs, cries and cares. All these —
cognitive/affective qualities of man, his unique
neshama, personality and spiritual mission in this
world — were breathed into Adam by God at creation.
And man's challenge in living is to use his God-given
talents and abilities to achieve his mission.

God breathed this *neshama*, the spiritual core of
man's existence, into man in the Garden of Eden. At
the dawn of creation, this *neshama* was one entity embodied in a bisexual Adam. With the formation of Eve
from Adam's body, man's soul, too, was separated to
be shared with his newly-created wife. Just as man can
only achieve the perfection of paradise by becoming
one again with his other half, so, too, does he attain
spiritual wholeness by reuniting with his soul-mate.
Since man's soul is the essence of his existence, it is
critical that it be matched with its preordained mate if
he is to succeed in his earthly mission.[5] We may now
better appreciate the response of one great sage who,
when asked what God is presently doing, replied: "He
is matching mates!" (*Vayikrah Rabbah* 8:1). It is no small
task, even for God, to select compatible soul-mates from
among all the souls that repose in heaven. Only a perfect match can create the combination for success.

The Talmud declares that it is "as difficult [for God] to pair them as it was to split the Red Sea!" (*Sota* 21). The Maharal delves into the meaning of this analogy. Water, he observes, is essentially one chemical entity, naturally cohesive, while man and woman are at two opposite poles, the spiritual and physical. The analogy is balanced: It is as difficult for God to unite two diverse entities as it was to divide one cohesive entity. To better appreciate the Maharal's interpretation, we need to understand the Talmud's perception of the roles of man and wife. A most critical passage (*Sotah* 17a) traces the etymology of man (איש) and woman (אשה). These words share two letters in common, אש, which spell fire. The word for man, however, contains an additional letter "yud" (י), while that for woman ends with another one, "hay" (ה). Together these two letters spell one of God's names. The Talmud observes that when man and woman dwell together in harmony, this two-letter name of God is joined and the *Shechinah* resides with them. But if there is strife between them, God is removed, as it were, from their midst; they then remain with fire, אש, a conflagration that destroys their home and family. A closer look at this beautiful analysis reveals more intriguing insights. The Talmud (*Menachos* 29b) comments on the verse in

Isaiah, "For with His name [Yud, Hay], God is the Rock of the Universe" (Isaiah 26:4), and construes the word for "rock" (צור) to mean "create" Accordingly, the Rabbis render the verse: "For with His Name, YAH, God created the Universe." The Talmud explains that with the "Yud" (י), the Almighty created the World to Come, while with the "Hay" (ה), He formed this world. Since the "Yud" is the letter contained in the word for man, it follows that he is primarily charged with a spiritual mission, the World to Come. Woman, however, was designated "the mother of all life" (Genesis 3:20) and the word for woman includes the "Hay" of God's Name, symbolizing the physical universe. By any measure, it would be difficult, if not impossible, to merge these two diametrically opposed worlds. Woman and man, in their respective roles, represent the eternal conflict between the physical and spiritual, between body and soul, between this world and the World to Come. They can only be united by an all-consuming force that will purge them of their egocentric concerns and bond them into one fire! Fire is both one of the most creative as well as destructive forces known to man. Fire provides us with the light, warmth and energy to power our civilization. Tragically, fire is also the blast of heat and blinding light emitted from nuclear bombs and modern weapons. When Adam takes that first tentative step to reach out to his physical half and when Eve, in turn, becomes the "helpmate" for her spiritual counterpart, then God bonds them in an ego-consuming fire. But if man and wife cannot bridge the spiritual and physical gap, their worlds will never meet and merge. Instead, they will clash and struggle, exploding in self-destruction. Since man and wife did not become one, they fail to become a creative force like God. Ultimately, they remain apart at opposite poles; their unchanneled flames run amock, consuming their own masters.

In the *Sheva Brachos*, the Seven Benedictions which we recite in honor of the bride and groom, we wish: "Truly rejoice, beloved friends, as the Creator caused you to rejoice before in a Garden of Eden," It is our hope and prayer that bride and groom, husband and wife, will return as lovers to paradise, where they will become one again. They will cleave together in body and become the perfect Adam, a proxy of God on earth, a merging of all the masculine and feminine forces. In their return to Eden, these two soul-mates, who were half, now become whole. These beloved friends, in affection and joy, reunite, bringing together body and soul, the physical and the spiritual, this world and the World to Come. Now one, they are at last ready to fulfill their mission on earth and become the parents of the next generation.

---

1. Rashi on 2:18 notes: "They [the creatures] should not say there are two [Divine] powers—God alone in the heavens without a partner and man on the earth without a mate." The meaning of this ambiguous comment is elucidated at its source in the Midrash: "The Holy One, Blessed be He, says: 'I am alone in My world, and he [Adam] is alone in his. I do not procreate; neither does he. All the creatures will say that since man does not procreate [and, like God, may be eternal], man created us.' Therefore it is written, 'It is not good for man to be alone' so that they will not say, there are two Divinities [lit., authorities]." *(Bereishis Rabbah)*. This Midrash seemingly contradicts the Talmudic concept *(Brachos* 61a) that man was originally created with the ability to self-propagate. Rashi's interpretation also stands in marked contrast to others' (Ramban, Or HaChaim) which are based on the Talmudic concept; see, however, Mizrachi who maintains that Rashi follows the plainer meaning of the text.

2. Note Ramban and Or HaChaim on 2:18. The latter explains, at great length, why God had originally created Adam as a bisexual creature and later found it necessary to remove his feminine half; in the process, he raises and resolves a number of major issues.

3. The Or HaChaim, *ibid.,* treats the issue of why God first saw that Adam's creation without a mate was "very good" (1:31) but later declared "it is not good for man to be alone!" (2:18). I would humbly suggest another thesis. God created the world, in general, and man, in particular, as a

manifestation of His kindness, *chesed:* "the world was created out of *chesed*" (Psalms 89:3). Obviously, God does not need man for His own existence; if this were so, if God would be somehow dependent on man for anything, it would imply that God is imperfect, which is clearly impossibile.

Thus, God created man for man's own benefit, as a kindness to him. But all creation would be for naught if the world did not recognize the source of its existence, the selfless kindness of God. Man, and only man, endowed with the highest form of intelligence, can truly recognize God's *chesed* and properly express appreciation to Him.

Man, as a proxy for God in the physical world, must embody the quality of *chesed*, showering it on the lower creatures. But no animal could reciprocate man's kindness toward it, or even properly express its gratitude. As a result, Adam, though completely self-contained, felt totally alone. He had no equal to relate to, no one who could recognize and appreciate his *chesed*. God, too, saw that Adam could no longer remain alone; he needed a counterpart to complement him, to receive and reciprocate his kindness. And so God created Eve from Adam.

4. Or HaChaim, Genesis 2:18.

5. *Zohar* 1:85, cited in *Pirkei Zohar*, pp. 47-49, and pp. 183-187.

GLOSSARY

Adar: the sixth month of the Jewish year, generally corresponding to February or March.

Av: the eleventh month of the Jewish year, generally corresponding to July or August.

"Be fruitful and multiply": the first commandment of the Torah, in which man is told to propagate and fill the world with his increase (children).

defilement: spiritual impurity; e.g., one who comes in contact with a corpse is considered to be in a state of defilement.

establishing a cycle: the recurrence of the menses three times in a specified pattern. This pattern, once established by the recurrence of the menses thrice, is referred to as a "regular cycle."

examination cloth (lit., 'checked cloth'): a soft, white cloth pre-checked and found free of any spot. This cloth may be used for an internal examination.

flow (lit., 'days of seeing'): menstruation.

halachah (lit., 'step'): the final decision of the Rabbis as transcribed in the Talmud and subsequent Judaic legal codes.

halachic authority: an expert in the area of halachah.

Havdalah candle (lit., 'separation candle'): the candle used in the ceremony by which the Shabbos is ushered out.

Hebrew calendar: the lunar calendar. The calendar year contains 12 months: Tishre, Heshvan, Kislev, Tevet, Shevat, Adar, Nisan, Iyar, Sivan, Tammuz, Av, and Elul, with the 29-day intercalary month of Adar Sheni added after Adar seven times in every 19-year cycle. A year where the month of Adar Sheni is added is referred to as a leap year. The beginning of the civil year coincides with the month of Tishre.

Heshvan: the second month of the Jewish year, generally corresponding to September or October.

immersion: the ritually prescribed act of dipping oneself in a *mikvah*.

interim of purity examination (lit:. 'stoppage of purity'): the examination of the vaginal tract made in the interim between the days of the flow and the seven clean days.

intermediate days of a holiday: The days between the first and last days of the Sukkoth (Tabernacles) and Pesach (Passover) holidays. On these days, unlike the first and last days of the holiday, certain types of work are permissible.

internal examination (lit., 'inspection'): a digital examination of the vaginal tract.

irregular cycle: menses, the beginning of which vary significantly and for which no specific patterns have been established.

Iyar: the eighth month of the Jewish year, generally corresponding to April or May.

Kiddush (lit., 'sanctification'): the blessing recited, usually over wine, on the Sabbath or other holy day.

Kislev: the third month of the Jewish year, generally corresponding to October or November.

leap year: see Hebrew calendar.

mikvah (lit., 'a gathering [of water'): a bath containing forty *se'ahs* of undrawn water.

niddah: a woman during the period of her menstruation. This period concludes with seven clean days and an immersion in a *mikvah*.

Nisan: the seventh month of the Jewish year, generally corresponding to March or April.

preparations for immersion: the removal of any separations from the *niddah's* person prior to immersion.

preparations for the seven clean days: the cleansing of the vaginal area and inspection thereof for signs of menstrual bleeding and the provision of stain-free clothing and linens at the beginning of the seven clean days.

Purim seudah: the main meal served on the holiday of Purim. This festival is celebrated on the fourteenth or fifteenth of Adar.

purity: spiritual cleanliness, e.g., a *niddah* who immerses herself in a *mikvah*, returns to a state of purity.

regular cycle: see establishing a cycle.

ritualarium: a building housing a *mikvah*.

safeguards: the laws prohibiting sexual intimacy during the *niddah* period.

se'ah: measure of capacity equal to 24 *logs.* A *log* is a liquid measure equal to the space occupied by six eggs, c 549 cubic centimeters.

separations: certain substances or articles, such as tight jewelry or braids, preventing contact between one's body and the water of the *mikvah,* which render the immersion invalid.

seven clean days: seven consecutive days wherein no menstrual bleeding whatsoever takes place.

Shabbos: the seventh day of the week, wherein all manner of work is forbidden.

Sivan: the ninth month of the Jewish year, generally corresponding to May or June.

spot: a discoloration found on an examination cloth possibly resulting from menstrual bleeding. Note *stain* below.

stain: a discoloration found on a woman's undergarments or linen, possibly resulting from menstrual bleeding. Note *spot* above.

Tammuz: the tenth month of the Jewish year, generally corresponding to June or July.

Tisha B'Av: the ninth day of the month of Av commemorating the destruction of both temples.

Tishre: the first month of the Jewish year, generally corresponding to September or October

Yom Kippur: the Day of Atonement observed on the tenth day of Tishre.

Index

. . . .

*Mikvah Directory—United States**

Alabama

Congregation Agudath Israel
3525 Cloverdale Rd.
Montgomery, AL 36111
334-281-7998 or 281-7394

Knesseth Israel Synagogue
3225 Montevallo Rd.
Birmingham, AL 35223
205-879-1664 or 871-3141
(Private)

Alaska

Congregation Lubavitch
  Shomrei Ohr
1210 East 26th Ave.
Anchorage, AK 99508
907-279-1200

Arizona

Mikvah Society
515 E. Bethany Home Rd.
Phoenix, AZ 85012
602-277-7479

Mikveh Perach Yisroel
By Cong. Chofetz Chaim
Tucson, AZ 85711
Esther Becker - 520-591-7680

Young Israel Synagogue
2442 E. 4th St.
Tucson, AZ 85719
602-881-7956 (Private)

Arkansas

Congregation Agudath Achim
7901 W. 5th St.
Little Rock, AR 72205
501-225-1683

California

Mikvah Taharas Israel
2520 Warring St.
Berkeley, CA 94704
415-848-7221

Teichman Mikvah Society
12800 Chandler Blvd.
North Hollywood, CA 91607
818-506-0996 or 763-0560

Mikvas Chana
24412 Narbonne Ave.
Lomita, CA 90717
213-326-3886 or 326-8234

Mikvah Chaya V'Sarah Leah
3847 Atlantic Ave.
Long Beach, CA 90807
310-427-1360

Los Angeles Mikvah:
  Mikvat Esther
9548 W. Pico Blvd.
Los Angeles, CA 90035
213-550-4511

---

*Courtesy of the Union of Orthodox Jewish Congregations.
For an international directory, go to www.ou.org.

Bais Yehuda
360 N. La Brea Ave.
Los Angeles, CA 90036
213-939-4297 Entrance in rear
alley (guard on duty)

Beth Jacob Community Mikvah
3778 Park Blvd.
Oakland, CA 94610
510-482-1147 No Attendant

Chabad House
3070 Louis Rd.
Palo Alto, CA 94303
415-424-9800

Knesseth Israel Torah Center
1024 Morse Ave.
Sacramento, CA 95864
916-481-1158 or 481-1159

Mikvah Israel
5160 La Dorna
San Diego, CA 92115
619-287-6411

Mikvah Israel: B'nai David of
San Francisco
3355 Sacramento St.
San Francisco, CA 94118
415-921-4070 (Private)

Chabad of Marin
1150 Idylberry Rd.
Sab Rafael, CA 94903
415-492-1666

Chabad of Palm Springs
425 Avenida Ortega
Palm Springs, CA 92264
619-325-3212

Abraham Dayan Mikvah -
  Chabad
18181 Burbank Blvd.
Tarzana, CA 91356
818-758-3836 (Mikvah)

The La Jolla Mikvah
@Congregation Adat Yeshurun
8625 La Jolla Scenic Drive North
La Jolla, CA 92037
(858) 535-1072

Colorado
Mikvas Chana - Chabad
2835 E. Platte Ave.
Colorado Springs, CO 80909
719-475-8910 (Office)

Mikvah of Denver
1404 Quitman
Denver, CO 80204
303-893-5315 or 623-1659

Mikvah of East Denver
  (Tomer Devorah)
295 S. Locust Street
Denver, CO 80224
303-320-6633

Connecticut
Mikvah Israel
1326 Stratfield Rd.
Fairfield, CT 06432
203-374-2191

New Haven Mikvah Society
86 Hubinger St.
New Haven, CT 06511
203-387-2184
Call for appointment

Beth Israel of Norwalk/
  Westport
40 King St.
Norwalk, CT 06851
203-866-0534 or 852-9041

Congregation Brothers of Joseph
2 Broad St.
Norwich, CT 06360
203-887-3777 or 889-5776

Congregation Agudath Sholom
301 Strawberry Hill Ave.
Stamford, CT 06902
203-358-2270 or 358-0466
(Private)

Congregation B'nai Shalom
Synagogue
135 Roseland Ave.
Waterbury, CT 06710
203-754-4159 or 753-1206

Mikvah Beth Israel
61 N. Main St.
West Hartford, CT 06107
203-521-9446

Delaware
Mikvah Chaya Mushka -
  Chabad
1306 Grinnell Rd.
Wilmington, DE 19803
302-478-4400

Florida
Boca Raton Synagogue
7900 Montoya Circle
Boca Raton, FL 33433
407-394-5854

Young Israel of Hollywood
3291 Stirling Rd.
Ft. Lauderdale, FL 33312
305-963-3952 (Mikvah) or 966-
7877 (Synagogue)

Mikvah Etz Chaim
10167 San Jose Blvd.
Jacksonville, FL 32257
904-262-3565

Mikvah Yisroel of Orlando
708 Lake Howell Rd.
Maitland, FL 32751
407-740-8770 (Private)

Mikvah Center
2530 Pine Street Dr.
Miami Beach, FL 33139
305-672-3500

Mikvah Dej
225 37th St.
Miami Beach, FL 33140
305-538-0070 or 674-8204

Mikvah Blima of North Dade
1054 Miami Gardens Dr.
North Miami Beach, FL 33179
305-949-9650 or 653-8553

Mikvah Israel of Tampa Bay
14908 Pennington Rd.
Tampa, FL 33624
813-962-2375 (Private) or
963-0706 (Private)
West Palm Beach, FL
Closest Mikvah - Boca Raton, FL

Georgia

Congregation Beth Jacob
1855 La Vista Rd. NE
Atlanta, GA 30329
404-728-0441 (Mikvah) or
728-0551 (Synagogue)

B'nai Torah
700 Mt. Vernon Hwy.
Atlanta, GA 30328
404-257-0537

Chabad Center and Bet Tefilah
Synagogue
5065 High Point Rd.
Atlanta, GA 30342
404-843-2464 -appointment -
255-9001

Congregation Adas Yeshurun
935 Johns Rd.
Augusta, GA 30904
404-733-9491

Congregation Bnai Brith Jacob
5444 Abercorn
Savannah, GA 31405
912-354-9619 (Private) or
354-7721

Hawaii

Aloha Jewish Chapel at
Makalapa Gate
Naval Station Box 47
Pearl Harbor, HI 96860
808-471-0050 for information

Illinois

Chicago Mikvah Association
3541 W. Peterson Ave.
Chicago, IL 60659
312-509-0900

Touhy Mikvah of Chicago
Mikvah Association
3110 W. Touhy Ave.
Chicago, IL 60645
312-274-7425

Congregation Yehuda Moshe
4721 W. Touhy Ave.
Lincolnwood, IL 60646
708-675-8510 (Private) or
674-6272 (Private)

Congregation Agudas Achim
3616 N. Sheridan Rd.
Peoria, IL 61604
309-688-4800

Tri-City Jewish Center
2715 30th St.
Rock Island, IL 61201
309-788-3426

Indiana

Congregation Bnai Torah
6510 Hoover Rd.
Indianapolis, IN 46260
317-253-5253 -
Mikvah Hotline - 317-475-1429

Hebrew Orthodox Congregation
3207 High St.
South Bend, IN 46614
219-291-4239, 291-9014,
287-7147 (Private)

Iowa

Beth El Jacob Synagogue
954 Cummins Pkwy.
Des Moines, IA 50312
515-274-1551

Jewish Federation of Sioux City -
   Cong. Beth Shalom
815 - 38th St.
Sioux City, IA 51104
712-258-0618

Kansas

Mikvah Chana - Chabad
6201 Indian Creek Dr.
Overland Park, KS 66207
913-649-7770 (Private -
   Esther Friedman) 649-4852

Kehilath Israel Synagogue
10501 Conser
Overland Park, KS 66212
913-642-1880

Ahavath Achim Hebrew
Congregation
1850 N. Woodlawn
Wichita, KS 67208
316-685-1339

Kentucky

Louisville Vaad Hakashruth
3700 Dutchmans La.
Louisville, KY 40205
502-451-3122

Louisiana

Beth Israel Synagogue
7000 Canal Blvd.
New Orleans, LA 70124
504-283-4366 (Shul)

Mikvah Chaya Mushka -
   Chabad
7037 Freret St.
New Orleans, LA 70118
504-866-5342 (Private)

Maine

Mikvah
336 Pine St.
Bangor, ME 04401
207-945-5940
(Private - Rabbi Isaacs)

Shaaray Tphiloh Synagogue
76 Noyes St.
Portland, ME 04103
207-773-0693

Maryland

Bais HaMidrash
   Khal Arugas Habosem
6615 Park Heights Ave.
Baltimore, MD 21215

Mikvah
3207 Clarks Lane
Baltimore, MD 21215
410-764-1448

Lubavitch Mikvah -
   Mikvah Ateres Yisroel
11621 Seven Locks Rd.
Potomac, MD 20854
301-299-0144

Mikvah
8901 Georgia Ave.
Silver Spring, MD 20910
301-565-3737

Silver Spring Jewish Center
1401 Arcola Ave.
Silver Spring, MD 20902
301-649-4425 or 649-2799

Massachusetts
Daughters of Israel
101 Washington St.
Brighton, MA 02135
617-782-9433

Lubavitch Mikvah
239 Chestnut Hill Ave.
Brighton, MA 02135
617-782-8340, 562-0141

Mikvah Chaya Mushka
9 Burlington St.
Lexington, MA 02173
607-787-2667 or 862-6626

Mikvah Israel
1104 Converse St.
Longmeadow, MA 01106
413-567-1607 or 736-1009

Montefiore Mikvah
36 Academy Dr.
Lowell, MA 01851
508-459-9400 or 458-8797

Mikvah Bnot Yisroel -
Congregation Ahabat Sholom
151 Ocean St.
Lynn, MA 09102
617-595-0080 (Mikvah) or
593-9255 (Shul)

Chevrat Nashim - Mikvah
Organization of the South Shore
9 Dunbar St.
Sharon, MA 02067
617-784-7444

Worcester Mikvah
4 Huntley St.
Worcester, MA 01602
508-756-6483 (Private) or
752-7749 (Private)

Michigan
Chabad House
715 Hill St.
Ann Arbor, MI 48104
313-995-3276

Chabad
5385 Calkins
Flint, MI 48532
810-733-3779 OR 230-0770

Chabad House
2615 Michigan NE
Grand Rapids, MI 49506
616-957-0770 or 949-6788

Mikvah Israel
15150 W. Ten Mile Rd.
Oak Park, MI 48237
248-967-5402

Beis Chabad Torah Center
5595 W. Maple Rd.
West Bloomfield, MI 48033
810-855-6170

Minnesota
Ritualarium Society Knesseth
Israel Synagogue
4330 W. 28 St.
Minneapolis, MN 55416
612-926-3829 or 926-3185

Mikvah Chana
730 Second St. SW
Rochester, MN 55902
507-288-5007

Mikvah Association
1516-1/2 Randolph Ave.
St. Paul, MN 55105
612-698-6163 or 698-1298

Missouri
Taharath Israel of St. Louis -
  Sylvia Green Mikvah
4 Millstone Campus
St. Louis, MO 63146
314-569-2770

Nebraska
Rose Blumkin Home
333 South 132 St.
Omaha, NE 68154
402-556-6288 (Shul)

Nevada
Chabad Mikvah
1254 Vista Dr.
Las Vegas, NV 89102
702-224-0184 or 259-0770

Shaarei Tefila Mikvah
1331 S. Maryland Pkwy.
Las Vegas, NV 89104
702-384-0772 (Private - Rabbi)

New Hampshire
Congregation Machzikei Hadath
Lewis Hill Rd.
Bethlehem, NH 03574
603-869-3336 (Private)

New Jersey
The Mikvah of Central Jersey/
  Twin Rivers
639 Abbington Drive
East Windsor, NJ 08520
Contact Ruthie Chinn
609-443-1599 for appointments

Fair Lawn Mikveh -
  Cong. Shomrei Torah
19-10 Morlot Ave.
Fair Lawn, NJ 07410
201-796-0350

Park Mikvah
112 South First Ave. South
Highland Park, NJ 08904
908-249-2411

Mikvah
1101 Madison Ave.
Lakewood, NJ 08701
908-370-1666 or 370-8909

Congregation Zichron Shneur
280 Oak Knoll Rd.
Lakewood, NJ 08701
908-363-6330

Congregation Zichron Yoel
1014 Lawrence Ave.
Lakewood, NJ 08701
908-363-3830

Mikvah Israel of Atlantic County
8223 Fulton Ave.
Margate, NJ 08402
609-822-9797

Mikvah Bais Chana - Lubavitch
93 Lake Rd.
Morristown, NJ 07960
201-292-3932

Mikvah
Near Gershel Ave.
Norma, NJ 08347
609-692-7176 (Private)

Shore Area Mikvah
201 Jerome Ave.
Oakhurst, NJ 07755
732-531-1712

Mikvah Yisroel of Passaic-Clifton
244 High St.
Passaic, NJ 07055
201-778-3596

Congregation Shaarey Tefiloh
15 Market St.
Perth Amboy, NJ 08861
201-826-2977

Mikvah Yisroel - Chabad
731 Princeton Kingston Rd.
Princeton, NJ 08540
609-252-0114 or 252-0124

Mikvah Association
1726 Windsor Rd.
Teaneck, NJ 07666
201-837-8220

Essex County Ritualarium
717 Pleasant Valley Way
West Orange, NJ 07052
201-731-1427

Sons of Israel
720 Cooper Landing Rd.
Cherry Hill, NJ 08002
609-667-9700 or 667-3515

Young Israel of East Brunswick
193 Dunhams Corner Rd.
East Brunswick, NJ 08816
908-257-4121

Bruriah High School
35 North Ave.
Elizabeth, NJ 07208
201-352-5048

Englewood Mikvah Association
89 Huguenot St.
Englewood, NJ 07631
201-567-1443

Lubavitch on the Palisades
48 Piermont Road
Tenafly, NJ 07670
201-816-0440

New Mexico
Pardes Yisroel
1178 Calle Royale
Santa Fe, NM 87501
505-986-2091
(Private - Chana Katz)

New York

Aitz Chaim
708 Mace Ave.
Bronx, NY 10467
718-798-6173

Mikvah
3708 Henry Hudson Pkwy.
Riverdale, NY 10463
212-549-8336

Mikvah of Canarsie
1221 Remsen Ave.
Brooklyn, NY 11236
718-763-5902 or 763-6812

Crown Heights Mikvah
1506 Union St.
Brooklyn, NY 11213
718-604-8787

Mikvah Divrei Chaim
1249 52nd St.
Brooklyn, NY 11219
718-972-9678

Mikvah Israel of Bensonhurst
48 Bay 28 St.
Brooklyn, NY 11214
718-372-9563, 373-8887 (Private)

Mikvah Israel of Boro Park
1351 46th St.
Brooklyn, NY 11219
718-871-6866

Mikvah Israel of Boro Park
1574 58th St.
Brooklyn, NY 11219
718-871-0669

Mikvah Israel of Boro Park
4623 18th St.
Brooklyn, NY 11219
718-436-5140

Mikvah Israel of Brighton
245 Neptune Ave.
Brooklyn, NY 11235
718-769-8599

Kehilas Yaakov
115 Rutledge
Brooklyn, NY 11211
718-624-9262

Mikvah Nachlas Tzvi
3210 Kings Hwy.
(Entrance on Ave. N)
Brooklyn, NY 11234
718-338-3545

Congregation and Yeshiva
    Hamaor
5010-12 18th Ave.
Brooklyn, NY 11204
718-633-7724

Mikvah Yisroel of Flatbush
1980 Avenue L
(Corner Ocean Ave.)
Brooklyn, NY 11230
718-258-7704
Handicapped Facilities Available

Ritualarium of East Flatbush
340 E. 52nd St.
Brooklyn, NY 11203
718-771-5842 (Private)

Sephardic Mikvah Israel
810 Avenue S
Brooklyn, NY 11223
718-339-4600

Yetev Lev D'Satmar
212 Williamsburg St.
Brooklyn, NY 11211
718-387-9388

Young Israel of Bedford Bay
2113 Haring St.
Brooklyn, NY 11229
718-332-4120, 646-3253 (Private)

Taharath Israel of Flatbush, Inc.
1013 E. 15 St.
Brooklyn, NY 11230
718-377-9813

Jewish Women's Club
234 West 78th St.
New York, NY 10024
212-799-1520

Mikvah Beth Avraham
163 E. 69th St.
New York, NY 10021
212-472-3968

Mikvah of East Side
313 E. Broadway
New York, NY 10002
212-475-8514

Mikvah of Washington Heights
4351 Broadway
New York, NY 10033
212-923-1100

Mikvah
1121A Sage St.
Far Rockaway, NY 11691
718-327-9727

Congregation of Georgian Jews
  from Russia
63-04 Yellowstone Blvd.
Forest Hills, NY 11375
718-897-9370 or 718-997-9077

Congregation Mikvah Israel
71-11 Vleigh Place
Kew Garden Hills, NY 11367
718-268-6500

Community Mikvah -
  Young Israel of Staten Island
835 Forest Hill Rd.
Staten Island, NY 10314
718-494-6704

Mikvah Israel of Willowbrook
98 Rupert Ave.
Staten Island, NY 10314
718-494-3359 (Private)

Young Israel of Eltingville
374 Ridgewood Avenue
Staten Island NY 10312
718-948-8825

Bnos Israel, Inc.
340 Whitehall Rd.
Albany, NY 12208
518-437-1303 or 453-9406

Belle Harbor
  Community Mikvah
511 Beach 129 St.
Belle Harbor, NY 11694
718-945-4420 or 318-5712

Congregation Ohab Zedek
134-01 Rockaway Beach Blvd.
Belle Harbor, NY 11694
718-945-4420

Beth David Synagogue
39 Riverside Dr.
Binghamton, NY 13905
607-722-1793

Buffalo Ritualarium
1248 Kenmore
Buffalo, NY 14216
716-875-8451 (Evenings only)

Suffolk Mikvah Inc.
74 Hauppauge Rd.
Commack, NY 11725
516-462-6075

Jewish Home of
  Central New York
4101 E. Genesee St.
Dewitt, NY 13214
315-446-6194 or 424-0363

Congregation Ezrath Israel
Rabbi Eisner Square
Ellenville, NY 12428
914-647-4472 (Evening)
or 647-6846

North Shore Mikveh Association
26 Old Mill Rd.
Great Neck, NY 11023
516-487-2726

Congregation South Shore
1156 Peninsula Blvd.
Hewlett, NY 11557
516-295-2995

Mikvah
209 N. Meadow St.
Ithaca, NY 14850
607-257-7379 or 273-5394

Mikvah Taharas Israel
37 Lincoln Place
Liberty, NY 12754
914-292-6677

Yisroel Meir and Devorah
Wakslak Long Beach Mikvah
280 East Penn Street
(cor. Monroe Boulevard)
Long Beach, New York 11561
(516) 897-4665

Congregation Yetev Lev
60 Acres Rd.
(Bet. Forest and Bakertown)
Monroe, NY 10950
914-782-2643

Mikvah of Concord
19 Bartlett Rd.
Monsey, NY 10952
914-425-8598

Mikvah Israel
4 Maple Leaf Rd.
Monsey, NY 10952
914-356-1000

Mikvah of Rockland County
238 Viola Road
Monsey, NY 10952
845 371-0211

Mikvah
16 North St.
Monticello, NY 12701
914-794-6757 or 794-8470

Yeshiva Farm Settlement Mikvah
Pines Bridge Rd.
Mount Kisco, NY 10549
914-666-0211, 666-3652

Mikvas Chaya
315 N. Main St.
New City, NY 10956
914-638-9398

Mikvah Association of
  Oceanside
3397 Park Ave.
Oceanside, NY 11572
516-766-3242

Mikvah Association of
  Long Island
97 Southern Parkway
Plainview, NY 11803
516-933-3215

Shomrei Israel Synagogue
18 Park Ave.
Poughkeepsie, NY 12603
914-454-2890
or 452-7583 (Private)

Beth Hatvilah
27 St. Regis Dr. North
Rochester, NY 14618
716-442-0245

Congregation Mikvah Israel
30 Lafayette St.
Saratoga Springs, NY 12866
518-584-6338

Young Israel of Scarsdale
1313 Weaver St.
Scarsdale, NY 10583
914-472-0946 (Private)
or 636-8686

New Square
33 Truman Ave.
Spring Valley, NY 10977
914-354-6578

Congregation Anshei Hashoran
Thompkins St.
Tannersville, NY 12485
518-589-5830

Chaya Mushka Mikvah -
  Chabad
2306 15 St.
Troy, NY 12180
518-274-5572 (Private)

Zvi-Jacob Synagogue
110 Memorial Pkwy.
Utica, NY 13501
315-724-8357 or 724-1078
(Private)

Mikvah Association
   of Nassau County
775 Hempstead Ave.
West Hempstead, NY 11552
516-489-9358

Mikveh Shearith Hapletah
Route 52
Woodbourne, NY 12788
914-434-5111

Mikvah
Maurice Rose St.
Woodridge, NY 12789
914-434-4987 or 434-8981

North Carolina
Lubavitch of North Carolina
6500 Newhall Rd.
Charlotte, NC 28270
704-366-3984

Congregation Shaarei Israel
7400 Falls of the Neuse Rd.
Raleigh, NC 27615
919-847-8986

Ohio
Mikvah
2479 S. Green Rd.
Beachwood, OH 44122
216-381-3170

Beth Tefillah
1546 Kenova Ave.
Cincinnati, OH 45237
513-821-6679 (Private) 761-0135

Mikvah
Taylor Rd.
Cleveland Heights, OH 44118
216-397-1040
or 371-4686 (Private)

Congregation Beth Jacob
1223 College Ave.
Columbus, OH 43209
614-237-1068 (Private)
or 237-8641

Mikvah
556 Kenwood Ave.
Dayton, OH 45406
513-274-1662 (Private)
or 277-7337

Etz Chaim Synagogue
3853 Woodley Rd.
Toledo, OH 43606
419-473-2401

Telshe Yeshiva
28400 Euclid Ave.
Wickliffe, OH 44092
216-585-0797

Greater Youngstown Area
Mikveh Association
3970 Logan Way
Youngstown, OH 44505
216-759-2167 or 759-1429

Oklahoma

Emmanuel Synagogue
900 NW 47 St.
Oklahoma City, OK 73118
405-528-2113

Mikvah Shoshana - Chabad
6622 S. Utica Ave.
Tulsa, OK 74136
918-493-7006

Oregon

Synagogue,
    The Halachic Minyan
2548 Willamette
Eugene, OR 97405
503-344-5096 (Private)

Jewish Ritualarium
1425 S.W. Harrison St.
Portland, OR 97201
503-224-3409

Pennsylvania

Mikvah
1834-1836 Whitehall St.
Allentown, PA 18104
215-433-6089

Philadelphia Mikvah Association
Wynnewood and Argyle Rds.
Ardmore, PA 19003
610-642-8679

Mikvah
3601 N. 4th St.
Harrisburg, PA 17110
717-234-0097 (Private)
or 232-2023

Ohev Zedek
3rd Ave. and Davis St.
Kingston, PA 18704
717-287-5793 (Private), 287-6336

Congregation Gemilas Chesed
1545 Ohio Ave.
Mckeesport, PA 15131
412-678-8859 (Shul), 678-2725

Philadelphia Mikvah Association
7525 Loretto Ave.
Philadelphia, PA 19111
215-745-3334

Jewish Women's League
2336 Shady Ave.
Pittsburgh, PA 15217
412-422-7110

Scranton Ritualarium
    Association Mikvah Yisroel
917-919 E. Gibson St.
Scranton, PA 18510
717-344-5138 or 347-9238
(Private)

Ohev Sholom
Cherry and Belmonts Sts.
Williamsport, PA 17701
717-322-7050 (Private)
    or 322-4209

Rhode Island

Jewish Community Center
401 Elmgrove Ave.
Providence, RI 02906
401-432-2291

South Carolina

Brith Sholom Beth Israel
182 Rutledge Ave.
Charleston, SC 29403
843-577-6599

Beth Shalom Synagogue
5827 N. Trenholm Rd.
Columbia, SC 29206
803-782-1831

Beth El Mikvah
404 Calhoun Rd.
Myrtle Beach, SC 29577
803-449-3956 or 448-0035

Tennessee

Beth Sholom Congregation
20 Pisgah Ave.
Chattanooga, TN 37411
615-894-0801

Anshei Sphard-Beth El Emeth
120 East Yates Rd. North
Memphis, TN 38120
901-682-1611

Baron Hirsch Congregation
400 S. Yates Rd.
Memphis, TN 38120
901-683-7485

Congregation Sherith Israel
3600 West End Ave.
Nashville, TN 37205
615-292-6614

Texas

Mikve Tahara
2101 Nueces
Austin, TX 78705
512-478-8222 or 472-3900

Congregation Tifereth Israel
10909 Hillcrest Rd.
Dallas, TX 75230
214-373-7536

Mikvah Chaya Mushka
6505 Westwind Dr.
El Paso, TX 79912
915-833-5711 (Private)
or 584-8218

Congregation Bnai Zion
805 Cherry Hill La.
El Paso, TX 79912
915-833-2222

Mikvah Taharas Yisroel
10900 Fondren
Houston, TX 77096
713-777-2000

United Orthodox Synagogue
9001 Greenwillow
Houston, TX 77096
713-723-3850

Congregation Rodfei Sholom
3003 Sholom
San Antonio, TX 78230
210-493-3557

Utah
Chabad-Lubavitch of Utah
1435 S 1100 E
Salt Lake City 84105
801-582-0220

Vermont
Mikvah Chaya Mushka
221 Summit St.
Burlington, VT 05401
802-658-7612 (Private)

Virginia
Congregation Adath Jeshurun
12646 Nettles Dr.
Newport News, VA 23606
757-930-0820

Congregation Bnai Israel
420 Spotswood Ave.
Norfolk, VA 23517
757-627-7358, 757-627-4582

Lubavitch Center
212 Gaskins Rd.
Richmond, VA 23233
804-740-2000

Young Israel of Richmond -
    Cong. Kol Emes
4811 Patterson Ave.
Richmond, VA 23226
804-353-5831
or 288-8816 (Private)

Washington
The Seattle Mikvah
5145 S. Morgan St.
Seattle, WA 98118
206-723-3644 , 517-7139
or 721-0970

West Virginia
Bnai Jacob Synagogue
1599 Virginia St.
Charleston, WV 25311
304-346-4722

Wisconsin
Mikvah Chaya Mushka
225 Campbell St.
Madison, WI 53711
608-251-8764 (Private)
or 231-3450

Congregation Beth Jehuda
2700 No. 54 St.
Milwaukee, WI 53210
414-445-7300 or 442-5730

Lubavitch House
3109 N. Lake Dr.
Milwaukee, WI 53211
414-961-2266 or 961-6100

Wyoming
Mt. Sinai Congregation
2610 Pioneer Ave.
Cheyenne, WY 82001
307-634-3052